21]

CW00841445

To be an
Overcomer

RAPHAEL FERNANDES

DEDICATION

For all brothers and sisters who desire more than the average but got the vision and are standing in our generation as true overcomers.

Raph, pastor, Vine - Fort Myers - FL 2016.

CONTENTS

ACKNOWLEDGMENTS

What is an overcomer?

We must be clear about eternal life and the participation of the Kingdom of Heaven. The Lord Jesus speaking of John the Baptist said that *"until now the Kingdom of Heaven is taken by force"* (Matthew 11:12). Only those who strive for it are able to take possession of it. Based on the words of this passage, some Christians have affirmed that we must do something more than believe to receive our salvation. They teach that if we do not do extra works we will be lost. This is the great misunderstanding between the Kingdom of Heaven and eternal life.

Eternal life is obtained by believing. As soon as we believe we receive it. It's a matter of receiving it. However, entering into the kingdom of heaven is not a matter of receiving but conquering it. The gospel of Matthew mentioned the phrase "kingdom of heaven" 32 times. Not one time does it says that we receive the kingdom by faith. How then, may one receive the kingdom?

Not everyone who says to Me, 'Lord, Lord,' shall enter the kingdom of heaven, but he who does the will of My Father in heaven. (Matthew 7:21)

The kingdom is a matter of works, it's a matter of living the life God has for us. It's a matter of being poor in spirit (Matt. 5:3). It's a matter of being persecuted for righteousness' sake (Matt. 5: 10). The kingdom it's a matter of being an overcomer. (Revelation 2 and 3).

God never tells us to seek to obtain eternal life. Once we believe, we are saved. However, the bible says that we should seek diligently to obtain the Kingdom.

Eternal life is received by grace. The reward is for the overcomers. Grace is given equally, by the Lord Jesus, to all those who believe in Him. The condition for salvation is faith in the Lord. Besides faith, there is no other condition, since the Son of God has already fulfilled all of the requirements. Man receives salvation through the righteousness of God. However, we cannot enter into the kingdom unless our righteousness exceeds that of the scribes and the Pharisees (Matthew 5:20). We see that the matter of eternal life is completely based on the work of the Lord Jesus but, the kingdom is based on man's works.

"Our burden is to edify a church of OVERCOMERS where every member is a minister and each house an extension of the church, thereby conquering our generation for Christ through life-groups that multiply"

I invite you in the next 21 days to invest your time and to get inspired by these short texts we have prepare for you. Join this journey on becoming an overcomer!

Revelation 2:7 (NKJV)
"...To him who overcomes I will give to eat from the tree of life, which is in the midst of the Paradise of God." '

Revelation 2:11 (NKJV)
"He who overcomes shall not be hurt by the second death."

Revelation 2:17 (NKJV)
"...To him who overcomes I will give some of the hidden manna to eat. And I will give him a white stone, and on the stone a new name written which no one knows except him who receives it."

Revelation 2:26 (NKJV)
"And he who overcomes, and keeps My works until the end, to him I will give power over the nations."

Revelation 3:5 (NKJV)
"He who overcomes shall be clothed in white garments, and I will not blot out his name from the Book of Life; but I will confess his name before My Father and before His angels."

Revelation 3:12 (NKJV)
"He who overcomes, I will make him a pillar in the temple of My God, and he shall go out no more."

Revelation 3:21 (NKJV)
"To him who overcomes I will grant to sit with Me on My throne, as I also overcame and sat down with My Father on His throne."

1
OVERCOMERS FAST

Daniel 9:3 (ESV)
Then I turned my face to the Lord God, seeking
him by prayer and pleas for mercy with fasting
and sackcloth and ashes.

Fasting is a practice very present in the whole Bible, but mainly in the lives of the heroes of faith who decided to have a different kind of hunger rather than a mere natural hunger.

Matthew 5:6 (ESV)"Blessed are those who
hunger and thirst for righteousness, for they shall
be satisfied."

They decided to restrain from food, pleasures, and other natural delights. They hungered for a period of time to make their senses more aware of God's direction, ignoring the urgencies of daily routine and constant distractions. Fasting and prayer requires a goal, a purpose.

There is nothing wrong with praying for personal causes or fasting for specific direction when we need to make a serious decision, but there is a better way to pray and fast. There are more noble reason to spend your time and effort in prayer.

Matthew 6:33 (ESV) "But seek first the kingdom of God and his righteousness, and all these things will be added to you."

Jesus is saying that when we take care of the Kingdom, He will take care of our personal problems. Many times we forget that Jesus has a purpose for the people He placed around us, our colleagues, roommates, coworkers, etc... God is challenging us, first of all, to be their intercessors.

In Daniel 9, we can see that Daniel was concerned for God's people in captivity and sought to know what God would do with them. When he discovered in the Scriptures why his people were in captivity, he began to intercede for them, confessing the sins of the nation and agreeing with God regarding them. Then, he pleaded with God for mercy and deliverance for them. We can see in Daniel 9:23 and 10:12 that on the very first day Daniel began interceding, God sent a messenger who had been withheld for twenty-one days until there was finally a breakthrough.

Maybe you do not see your friends as people of God, but they are. God chose them already. God chose them to be saved.

Acts 18:10 (ESV) "...for I am with you, and no one will attack you to harm you, for I have many in this city who are my people."

This is God speaking with Paul after he had tried sharing the gospel in the city of Corinth and failed the first time. He was persecuted and mistreated, and before Paul gave up God reminded him, *"I have many in this city who are my people."* God called them "my people," a people that was not His... yet.

In Daniel's story, God delivered His people because Daniel interceded for them. We need to hear from God for His people and intercede for God's will to be done in them. We need to persist in effective, fervent prayer until they have a breakthrough. God's hand is moved, His angels are sent and His provision is granted in response to our prayers.

Do you make time to get away and hear from God for His people and to intercede for them? There is nothing like having alone time with God to hear what He wants for His people. Make it a part of your busy schedule to spend quality time alone with God.

If we intend to stand as a church of overcomers, we need to follow what we see in the churches that prevailed in history. Let me take as a good example the largest church on earth: Yoido Full Gospel Church in South Korea.

An hour away from Yoido, the Prayer Mountain in Osanri is a key to understand the growth of the world's largest church. Since March 1973, the Prayer Mountain has been open 24 hours a day, 365 days a year to all the people who desire to go pray and fast for one or even a few days.

On any given day you will find approximately three thousand people praying in the main auditorium. Another large number can be found praying in the "grottoes of prayer" (tiny single rooms where you can only be on your knees) at the "Prayer Mountain." The passion of these Korean believers is very noticeable when they pray. They do it with all of their strength, and literally, with all of their voices. It's common to find people in 40-day fasting, drinking only water.

Why is this the largest church in the world and its outreach impossible to match? We will not find a complete answer without praying like them.

When we pray we understand the incredible power of it. We understand the key element of growth.

God does not need our fasting. We need God to intervene in our causes.

Pray now: *Heavenly Father, I confess that often I have not spent much quality time interceding for the people who were assigned to me. (Mention people that God is putting on your heart these days)*

Please, stir me up to pray more diligently. I stand in prayer and fasting. I stand as an overcomer. In Jesus' name. Amen.

2
OVERCOMERS PRAY DAILY

Luke 5:16 (NLT - with notes) " But Jesus often withdrew to the lonely places for prayer."

When we see Jesus praying we often ask ourselves, "why?". Was He not the Son of God? Was He not God in flesh? Was He not the "answered-prayer" incarnated? The most important question should be, if Jesus needed to spend time alone with His Father, how much more, then, do we?

He is our example. Luke 5:15 explains that Christ's fame was spreading, and the success of His ministry compelled Him to spend more time with God. *Matthew 8:20 (ESV) "And Jesus said to him, "Foxes have holes, and birds of the air have nests, but the Son of Man has nowhere to lay His head."*

Jesus did not even have enough time to sleep. In the midst of an increasingly busy ministry, He separated himself from the multitude for a quiet time. It seems there was a favorite prayer time for Jesus. *Mark 1:35 "Very early in the morning, while it was still dark, Jesus got up, left the house and went off to a solitary place, where he prayed."* Before the busyness of His day began, Jesus spent time with the Father. Here is a key we should not lose. It is not about the freshness of the morning, it is about not starting you daily routine without daily prayer. Overcomers understand that without a daily portion, daily bread and a daily fresh gulp of living water we will drown in weakness and fatigue.

It's interesting how often we look for entertainment as a form of resting, or sports as way to distract our minds. The truth is that there is no true rest in other places other than the presence of God. *Psalms 16:11 (ESV) "You make known to me the path of life; in your presence there is fullness of joy; at your right hand are pleasures forevermore."*

Daily devotional time is the single most important discipline in the Christian life. During that daily time, God transforms us, feeds us, and gives us new revelation. On the other hand, not spending sufficient time with God can bring the agony of defeat and tiredness. How often have we raced out of the house, hoping to accomplish a little bit more, only to return bruised, depressed, and hurt? When we start the day without spending time with our Lord, we lack power and joy to face the demands of life.

Joel Comiskey, in his research project with 700 cell leaders in eight countries, found out that the Life Group leader's devotional life is the most important variable for the success and growth of that cell. In other words, those cell leaders who spent more time in their daily devotional time were more likely to effectively lead their life group to multiplication than those who did not. He says, "During quiet times alone with the living God, the cell leader hears God's voice and receives His guidance. In those still moments, the leader understands how to deal with the constant talker, how to wait for a reply to a question, or how to minister to a hurting member of the group. Life Group leaders moving under God's guidance have an untouchable sense of direction and leadership. Group members respond to a leader who hears from God and knows the way. God brings success." The Bible teaches us of a lifestyle of prayer. *Thessalonians 5:16-17 (ESV) Rejoice always, pray without ceasing, give thanks in all circumstances.*

The truth is that no one will have such an experience if he does not separate a special moment of prayer and devotion every day. Some Christians resist the notion of setting apart daily time to seek God. Paul implores us to *"... pray in the Spirit on all occasions with all kinds of prayers and requests" (Ephesians 6:18)*. How can you have your mind and soul ready to respond to the Spirit, if you lack the discipline of prayer in secret with God?

Jesus says in Matthew 6:5-6 (ESV) *"And when you pray, you must not be like the hypocrites. For they love to stand and pray in the synagogues and at the street corners, that they may be seen by others. Truly, I say to you, they have received their reward. But when you pray, go into your room and shut the door and pray to your Father who is in secret. And your Father who sees in secret will reward you.*

These verses map out a specific time, set apart to seek the Father, a time to meditate on His Word, to listen to the Spirit's voice, to worship

Him, and intercede for others.

Reading the Bible everyday gives life. The Scripture was given to be kept in high regard, to feed our faith and reveal God's authority. Spend time with the Bible until it impacts you and truly touches your heart. It is not a matter of another Christian chore. (It is a matter of completely becoming an overcomer.) When you read let the words gain weight, let them have meaning.

The goal is to come out of our prayer and Bible reading moment inspired, encouraged and empowered. We are not looking to feel good for ourselves, but to become a sharper tool in God's hand. If God moves in your heart to make a call, to send a text message or to meet a person and express Christ, do it! Regardless of how much He reveals to you through Scripture to love your neighbor as yourself eventually, you will have to put your Bible aside and actually love him or her. So, dissect a passage, but focus on the application.

If your Bible reading does not convict you to close your bible and go love your neighbor, you are probably not reading it right. Do not abandon your Bible, but let God use His words to enable you to fulfill it. Approach the Bible with thirst and hunger. Return to the Bible everyday. When you do, pray that the Scripture stirs something in your heart. Coach Rolando Lamb, Founder/CEO of A-Game Elite Training System, said, "Overcomers and champions do daily what losers do occasionally."

Start today to walk in the path of the overcomers.

Pray now: *Jesus, You are the reason for my discipline. I want to pray for these friends who are still far from Your love (Mention their names). I ask that You create an opportunity today so I can share Your gospel. Father, I also pray for the seminarians of our church. Raise these students as missionaries for the nations. I am a participant of their call when I pray for them. In the name of Jesus, Amen.*

3

OVERCOMERS PRAY FOR OTHERS

Did you know that the sacrifice on the cross was for everyone on earth? Did you know that grace and mercy is for every person in our community? Did you know that the only thing that makes them far from God is a problem of faith? Finally, did you know that salvation is the gift of God?

Ephesians 2:8-9 For by grace you have been saved through faith. And this is not your own doing; it is the gift of God, not a result of works, so that no one may boast.

Here our prayer is essentially to let God's hand work on Earth convincing people to believe. We must learn to pray for people who are not saved and need to believe in the grace of God for themselves.

Paul the apostle was constantly asking for others to pray for him. In *Colossians 4:3-4, he says, "And pray for us, too, that God may open a door for our message, so that we may proclaim the mystery of Christ, for which I am in chains. Pray that I may proclaim it clearly, as I should.".* Notice that Paul's prayer request was not for himself. In the end he was asking for power, opportunities and boldness to preach the gospel to the lost. The goal is to reach the unbelievers.

Ephesians 6:18-19" praying at all times in the Spirit, with all prayer and supplication. To that end, keep alert with all perseverance ... for me, that words may be given to me in opening my mouth boldly to proclaim the mystery of the gospel"

Praying for each other is really important. I had one of the most incredible experiences with prayer recently. Thousands of faithful brother and sisters were praying for my family after the loss of my son. There were days that I could literally feel the prayers in my soul and sometimes even in my body. It was so powerful that sometimes I could even smell the scent of the prayers in the natural. Unfortunately, the majority of Christians do not believe that God will actually work in the life of the non-christian's friends when they pray, but He does! We must have an attitude of prayer for the unbelievers around us, because that's the only way God will move in their hearts to convince them.

Look in *Romans 15:30-33 " I appeal to you, brothers, by our Lord Jesus Christ and by the love of the Spirit, to strive together with me in your prayers to God on my behalf... and that my service ... may be acceptable ..."*

We pray to strive in evangelism. We pray so people can get saved. We pray so our LifeGroup meetings may be filled with the power of the Holy Spirit, convincing the hardheaded person to give in to God's love.

Again in *2 Corinthians 1:11 Paul says, "You*

also must help us by prayer, so that many will give thanks on our behalf for the blessing granted us through the prayers of many." Many will give thanks when we are empowered by prayer to bring them the good news of salvation.

Undoubtably, the main factor that has the greatest effect on whether a LifeGroup multiplies or not, is how much time the group leader spends praying for the LifeGroup members. The daily prayer by the leader for the members is essential for a healthy, growing group. Joel Comiskey's survey asked group leaders how much time they spent praying for the members of their group; the results confirmed that LifeGroup leaders who pray daily for their members are far more likely to multiply than those who pray for them only occasionally.

Praying daily for someone transforms your relationship with this person. God uses prayer to change your heart toward the people for whom you are interceding. Oneness, or unity, developes through the bonding power that prayer creates. Prayer opens our hearts to others and enables us to touch people at a deeper level. During this fasting time, try to pray for someone who maybe hurt you or has a relationship issue with you. Regularly, praying for someone can mend your broken relationship with that person. Through prayer, the healing balm of the Holy Spirit often breaks the strongholds of bitterness and unforgiveness. Prayer changes everything. Those who pray daily for their friends are more likely to become a minister, to become an overcomer.

We need to intercede for a world that doesn't know Jesus Christ. Here are some practical prayer strategies:

1- Leave one chair empty during each group

meeting to represent one or more unbelieving friends. Ask your group members to gather around the chair and pray for the salvation of the lost people in their sphere of influence.

2- Pair up the members of the LifeGroup who will pray daily for each other's lost friends. These partners can hold each other accountable.

3- The next meeting, ask for everyone in your LifeGroup to stand and pray aloud simultaneously for the salvation of specific non-Christian friends. It can be noisy, but it's powerful!

4- How about trying something more audacious. Invite your group to walk through the community where the meeting happens, praying for salvation to come to each home or apartment you walk past.

5- Create a "Most Wanted" poster and pray for the people on that poster. Many groups write the names of every relational contact on a large poster, so the whole group can intercede. Post it on the wall and pray for these people each week, making plans to connect them to the members between meetings. During the cell meeting, it's good to mention the names of those unbelieving friends in prayer.

6- Use every chance to create intercessory prayer for the unreached people of the community. Bring the profiles of unreached people groups that exist in your community (drug users, drug dealers, homosexuals, prostitutes, religious, depressed people,...), pass them out to group members, and then pray for people groups in smaller groups within the LifeGroup or together.

When you pray for unbelievers here are some tips. Raise your voice and pray for God to:
-Give them a hunger for Christ.
-Remove all barriers that are keeping them

from responding to Christ.
-For the Holy Spirit to make Jesus real to them.

Be creative! There is not one "right" way to pray, and flexibility always helps avoid the boredom of a routine. Get together with your group in an extra meeting just for prayer and let everyone raise their voices in unity. An atmosphere like that releases the faith of each one at a level that is impossible to not be moved and encouraged. How about starting right now?

Pray now: *Father, I understand that I can connect heaven on earth. So in Jesus' name I pray for those people who don't know Your grace and salvation. God, let me be aware of the opportunities that You are creating for the sharing of Your love. Today, I stand and pray for my pastors. I ask that they receive wisdom and power. Give them boldness to enter through the doors which You are opening for us as Your church. In the powerful name of Jesus. Amen.*

4
OVERCOMERS KNOW GRACE

*John 1: 14; 16; 17 "And the Word became flesh and dwelt among us, and we have seen His glory, glory as of the only Son from the Father, full of grace and truth...For from His fullness we have all received, **grace upon grace**. For the law was given through Moses; grace and truth came through Jesus Christ."*

Look what the Amplified version of these verses says,

"... we have all received one grace after another and spiritual blessing upon spiritual blessing and even favor upon favor and gift upon gift."

If we are going to talk about grace, it is kind of strange that John decided to mention the law here, but there are things that are only understood when you get the contrast. John used the law and Moses as a kind a blackboard that needed to be use to reveal and draw grace more clearly. Thus, to understand and enjoy grace you must know what the Law is.

In a nut shell, the law is trying to figure out a way to please God, all by yourself. On the other hand, grace, tells us that Jesus pleased God at the cross.

The law is all about merit. So, you can only receive anything good when you become worthy or deserve it. If you look in the Old Testament, you will notice that was the foundation of a relationship with God. Grace on the other hand, recognizes you worthy of hell, but God so loved you that He sent His Son to make you now worthy of Heaven. See *Isaiah 64:6 "We have all become like one who is unclean, and all our righteous deeds are like a polluted garment. We all fade like a leaf, and our iniquities, like the wind, take us away."* In other words, there is absolutely nothing good enough that we can ever do to make ourselves righteous before God. We accept it by grace alone.

The law says that God requires justice from men. Grace says that Jesus is God's justice available to everyone who believes. Jesus and you have real justice, you become just. I know many of us call ourselves believers in the gospel, but unfortunately many still hold to the old covenant of the law, trying their best to become righteous by the law, but Galatians 3:11 is so clear when it says, *"Now it is evident that no one is justified before God by the law, for 'The righteous shall live by faith.' "* We need to be very careful here, because we tend to emphasizes the self effort as the essential element of a godly life, but the Word of God is clear. It says that, if you do something, you should have FAITH, or TRUST in grace.

This does not mean I should not try to become a better person. The truth is that we do not accomplish transformation through an attempt to obey the law of Moses or the Ten Commandments. When we our minds are renovated by grace, we are empowered to fulfill God's will. Here in Romans 12:2 Paul reminds us the importance of being " ... *transformed by the renewal of your mind, ...*". Notice that transformation is a consequence of the revelation of grace, or as John mentioned: **grace upon grace.**

In addition, this growing in the revelation of grace is what makes us overcomers. *2 Corinthians 3:18 "And we all, with unveiled face, beholding the glory of the Lord, are being **transformed** into the same image **from one degree of glory to another**. For this comes from the **Lord who is the Spirit**.".*The Bible is clear that transformation is proportional to the experience with the glory of God, and the glory of God is His grace toward us.

The problem with the law is that it creates a sense of transformation, but it is only exterior, and since all that has an exterior appearance is temporal, the change does not endure. It is the flesh trying to change the flesh. It is not steadfast. Remember, God is Spirit (John 4:24), therefore the work of God is spiritual. Do not try to understand grace with your natural mind. It needs to be revealed in your spirit. Learn this: everything that God does is through His word and His Spirit. The law makes only an exterior appearance of change. There's no transformation of the heart. This kind of inside revolution happens only by the Spirit revealing grace to you. This is what Ephesians 3:16 says when Paul wrote, *"that according to the riches of His glory He may grant you to be strengthened with power through His Spirit in your inner being."*

Let's continue the comparison between law and grace. The law says, "Because of your sins you are cursed until your 3rd and 4th generation." *Exodus 20:5-6 "You shall not bow down to them or serve them, for I the Lord your God am a jealous God, visiting the iniquity of the fathers on the children to the third and the fourth generation of those who hate me."* Is there anyway to get out of this curse? Read *Galatians 3:10 " For all who rely on works of the law are under a curse; for it is written, "Cursed be everyone who does not abide by all things written in the Book of the Law, and do them."*

There is only one way out of all the curses of the law: not living under the law! He who lives under the law's dispensation, is always looking for special deliverance meetings, inner healing conferences, powerful prayer from the international preacher, etc... That is because people who are under the law are insecure as to whether or not they are under the curse. I believe in breaking curses and powerful prayer, but it was all done (It is finished! - John 19:30) on the day you accepted Christ. So, the only way to live under the curse is when you voluntarily decide to claim the law upon your life. When you still try to please God by your own effort, you will fall into the curse of the law.

The new covenant promises are: Isaiah 43:25 *"I, I am He who blots out your transgressions for my own sake, and I will not remember your sins".* Look now at what Hebrews 8:12 says: *"For I will be merciful toward their iniquities, and I will remember their sins no more."*

There is hope for you when you humbly accept your condition of incapability. *Galatians 3:13 "Christ redeemed us from the curse of the law by becoming a curse for us — for it is written, " Cursed is everyone who is hanged on a tree".* You get out of the Curse by trusting in the completeness of the redemption. You can delight in all the promises by relaying on grace alone.

If you depend on your merits, you are asking for curses instead of blessings. Some may be asking, "Why would someone choose the law rather than grace?" One of the reasons is that when you are guided by the law you just need to follow the norms and rules. You read the regulations and boast in yourself, not stopping to hear from the Spirit of God. You walk in the principle of the Tree of knowledge of good and evil (Genesis 2:17), which symbolizes independency from God and self leadership, instead of eating from the Tree of Life which represents the Life of Christ. Read Galatians 2:20-21 (ESV)

"...It is no longer I who live, but Christ who lives in me. And the life I now live in the flesh I live by faith in the Son of God, who loved me and gave Himself for me. I do not nullify the grace of God, for if righteousness were through the law, then Christ died for no purpose."

Stop today trying to improve yourself. Flesh cannot improve flesh. Only the Spirit can change you. Only the understanding of grace makes you a real overcomer. John 6:63 Jesus says *"It is the Spirit who gives life; the flesh is no help at all. The words that I have spoken to you are spirit and life."*

A very common experience that many brothers and sisters face when they are trying to live in obedience to the law, is that they discover that their obedience has no power to eliminate sin from their lives. The fact is that the law has no power to make someone righteous. In other words, even after you have tried your best, you will not be able to reach the point of overcoming the fleshly desires and habits. When you understand grace it's different. Grace gives power. Romans 6:14 affirms that " ... *sin will have no dominion over you, since you are not under law but under grace."* The power of Jesus to overcome sin manifests when we receive the revelation that we are under grace. We were made righteous. I do not obey God to become just, I obey because I am righteous; therefore, I can practice righteousness.

You have probably noticed when you read an internet post or any sign that says "Do not click this link" or "Prohibited to look inside" it seems that something inside of us is immediately awakens and a desire flourishes that make us want to click or look. Another problem with the Law is that you begin to be tempted by things that before it you paid no attention to. This is what Romans 7:8 confirms when it says *"but sin, seizing an opportunity through the commandment, produced in me all kinds of covetousness. For apart from the law, sin lies dead."* Remember Adam and Eve?

The law makes you afraid of God instead of fearing Him. The Israelites were always afraid of God's presence, due to the fact that they were never in complete accordance with the law. We are called by grace to enter with boldness before God's presence. *Hebrews 4:16 (ESV) "Let us then with confidence draw near to the throne of grace, that we may receive mercy and find grace to help in time of need".* The Israelites never imagined it would be possible to approach the presence of God, but we can even call Him ' Abba- Father'. We can come near to God because of grace.

If you don't understand that the law is a ministry of death, you won't receive the measure of life that grace has for you.

Read   2 Corinthians 3:7-8 *with my add on :*

*"Now if the ministry of death, carved in letters on stone **(the law)**, came with such glory that the Israelites could not gaze at Moses' face because of its glory, which was being brought to an end, will not the ministry of the Spirit have even more glory?"* I dare to answer YES, the ministry of the Spirit, the grace understanding will have so much more glory, because it releases life, not death!

Think with me: the message of the law does not need the revelation of the Spirit. It's pretty simple. If you behave well you will be blessed, and if you behave badly you will be cursed. Everyone knows that, even unbelievers have a good sense is of this knowledge. That's how all the religions systems are made, but Christianity is not about a group of moral rules that tries to improve you. Why should someone give their life to Christ in order to learn what they already know? They do not need conversion for this. Their own conscience accuses them.

True conversion means you are justified by grace and faith alone, not by works. It is not because you did something, but because God has already done it. You must have this revelation! Overcomers know grace. Overcomers walk by faith in grace.

Pray now: Father God, I repent for all those times I have spent trying to justify myself with my wrong idea of self righteousness. Now I can understand your Grace, and I pray that you remind me to walk by faith every day. I also ask You to give this revelation to my brothers and sisters, so our church will never run short of leaders anymore. Raise up Christians in this church who understand your grace, and are ready to guide others to this revelation. Amen.

5
OVERCOMERS OBEY

On church retreats one of the topics that is always preached about to the youth is obedience. Mainly because their audience is "rebellious teenagers" that are discovering the joy of the adult life. There is a very well known tale about a little boy in the church building who always played and ran during the service. His mother asked him to stop and to sit. After she asked him several times, as a good mother who does not want to correct her child, she looked him in the eyes and said to him "For the last time sit down now or you will be punished". Very upset the boy, who did not want to stop playing, finally sat down mumbling and said to his mother, "I'm sitting, but inside I'm standing up! "

It may be a funny story, but this child is expressing loud and clear what we often do. We obey outwardly, but our hearts are still rebellious. We keep standing, questioning and arguing with many words while the truth is placed before us, but we try bargaining to satisfy our flesh!

One day, I did not know how to teach my oldest son to listen and obey. At first, I tried to make some deals, "If you obey you will get such and such a thing... If you disobey you will lose this privilege." It did not work! I prayed and I asked the Lord to give me wisdom because he is growing and needs to have the revelation of what obedience actually means. I do not want to teach my son obedience through the law mindset. I want him to experience obedience as a result of grace.

The Lord asked me, "Why do you obey Me? Why do you have to obey Me as your God?" I realized that the answer to that question will also answer why it is so important to obey the Bible, or why we should follow the directions of our leaders and pastors. Some answers might come to your mind, "I have to obey because if I do not obey I will be punished. I must obey, because I have to follow the commandments of the Bible. I also know that everything I sow one day I will reap!" The truth is that we are surrounded by rules and laws such as, "you have to do this, you have to obey that." We grew up hearing "if you do not obey you will be punished like God did, in the Old Testament. After giving the commandments, He punished his people."

My answer to God was, "I obey You because I love You, Lord!" I felt the Holy Spirit reaffirming, "Much more than your love for Me, remember how much I love you!" Wow!! That was different. I then understood that it was not about my commitment and dedication to Him, but it was about His love towards me that inspired and motivated obedience in my heart. *1 John 4:19 "We love because He first loved us."*

Our conduct shows exactly what we believe. What we believe determines how we live.

Therefore, should I obey because I fear of the consequences and fear punishment, or should I obey because I understand that I am loved by God?

In Luke 6:46 says, *"Why do you call me 'Lord, Lord,' and not do what I tell you?"* In other words, if you say that you understand My love for you as your Lord, you should obey me. I recall asking my 9 years old son, "Son are you sure that daddy loves you?" He answered promptly, "Of course Dad!". I asked again, "Are you absolutely sure that Jesus loves you, son?" He once again said "Yes!". Then I explained, "That's why you should obey me. You are saying that you trust in my love and in my instruction, so obey me, son." I used the chance and I asked him, "Are you sure that Jesus loves you?" "Yes, I am sure! Jesus died on the cross for me!" He answered. I continued "If you are so sure that Jesus loves you, you should always trust that He has what's best for you, including the instructions that I give to you!"

We obey because we understand Jesus' love for us! Jesus loves us so much. I know and trust that, thus I obey. When my 2 year old son died in an accident, I had an even more profound revelation of God's love because in that overwhelming pain that I was feeling, I had the insight of what God also felt for me and for you! God suffered the greatest and most excruciating pain for me, a sinner who has no merit. Christ suffered and died out of love. What a passion He has. Yes, He loves me, I have no doubt about that!

We obey because we have revelation of His love for us! Without this revelation of His love, you will never be able to obey Him completely. There will always be something inside of you that will make you insurgent!

The apostle John, in his gospel, called himself

"the beloved disciple" (John 13:23). People think that maybe Jesus called him that, or maybe John was the favorite disciple of Jesus because he was a very intimate disciple. Actually, John called himself "the disciple, whom Jesus loved." John had the full revelation of Jesus' love for him. For the ones who see themselves as loved by Jesus, He will show many deep and intimate things, as He did with John. This beloved disciple saw heaven and received the book of Revelation. This is only for the very intimate and beloved disciples. This is only for the overcomers. The ones that obey because of love. The ones that feel loved will obey. For them there is a new level of revelation of eternity.

Overcomers understand that we do not belong to this earth. We are from heaven and while here on this earth, we will obey and fulfill the mission for which we are called! We obey as a result of trust. We know that our Father loves us, He has the best for us. He wants to make us more than conquerors!

Romans 8:37-39 " No, in all these things we are more than conquerors through Him who loved us. For I am sure that neither death nor life, nor angels nor rulers, nor things present nor things to come, nor powers, nor height nor depth, nor anything else in all creation, will be able to separate us from the love of God in Christ Jesus our Lord."

Pray now: *Father, my prayer today is that I can have the right idea of obedience, and not the wrong idea of inferiority that the world preaches. As Jesus obeyed in everything without being considered inferior, I also want to obey as a good son/daughter, to be approved and receive the reward You have for me. Also, let more of Your children have this revelation of obedience.*

I also pray for the authorities of our nation, that they can understand that they only have authority because of You, and that they can submit themselves to You in every decision they make. Amen.

6
OVERCOMERS ARE DISCIPLES

Matthew 16:24 (ESV) "Then Jesus told his disciples, "If anyone would come after me, let him deny himself and take up his cross and follow me."

Discipleship is not an easy subject to read, write, talk, and even less to live. It's time, as people of God, to step up into a new level of commitment. When we talk about engagement and commitment the words " deny yourself" and " renounce all" will come up, and it seems that Jesus relates these responses to anyone who stands as a disciple. Therefore not every Christian is a disciple. In other words , not every believer is an overcomer. Who is a disciple? Who is an overcomer?

Luke 14:33 (emphasis mine) "So therefore, any one of you who does not renounce all that he has cannot be my disciple."

Originally a disciple was the one who followed. Since Jesus is not always welcomed and well accepted, to be His disciple, in many circumstances, means not being welcomed as well and even being persecuted. Nevertheless, the main concept remains. You must follow someone to be his disciple. A practical way to follow Jesus is to look to someone who really follows Him above all else. Having a practical example will help us to truly follow Jesus and become real disciples. That's why Paul said *"Be imitators of me, as I am of Christ." 1 Corinthians 11:1.* Would you dare say, "Look at me and you will see Jesus?" Paul did it. You might think that Paul was a holy person without any flaws, right? Wrong!

He says in *Ephesians 3:8 "... I am the very least of all the saints, this grace was given, to preach to the Gentiles the unsearchable riches of Christ".* It is clear that he knew he wasn't perfect, or the greatest saint, although he also knew of the grace that was applied and sufficient for him. Here is an important key, without the understanding of grace we cannot become disciples.

The revelation of grace humbles us. Once you understand grace, you understand that it's not about you, but about Christ through you. Grace reveals our condition, having a lack of power. Grace displays who we really are. It's because of the grace that you had received, now you are able to be a disciple and make disciples.

Paul insists in 1 Corinthians 4:16-17 saying *'I urge you, then, be **imitators of me**. That is why I sent you Timothy, my beloved and faithful child in the Lord, to remind you of **my ways** in Christ, as I teach them everywhere in every church.'*

It's really important that you have your questions about discipleship answered. You need to be involved in the disciple making process. There is nothing more powerful to move you toward maturity and growth than an atmosphere of discipleship.

To begin this conversation, the message of the cross is the core value. 1 Corinthians 1:18 says *"For the word of the cross is folly to those who are perishing, but to us who are being saved, it is the power of God."* We are talking with saved people. To be a disciple, we must be sure of our salvation, however, we should not be willing to settled in our journey. We must desire more of God.

The word of the cross is necessary, because to follow your leader, to follow a discipler in your life, to follow these unpredictable people in your life you need to carry your cross. A relationship is a messy thing, and people are imperfect. This is why we need the cross in our relationship.

Discipleship, here in our country, may seem a little complicated, because the culture portrays people as individualists. A true disciple honors a discipler, and as a true disciple, he wants to be a disciple maker.

Paul was bold enough to say in Philippians 3:17, *"Brothers, join in imitating me, and keep your eyes on those who walk according to the example you have in us.".* When we begin our walk with Jesus, we don't have a clear image of how He actually lived, dealing with daily life routines and decisions. You can try to interpret the gospel and translate the two thousand years old context in our post-modern culture, but it's really hard to know what kind of Facebook post Jesus would post. You need someone to encourage you, to speak in your life, and to help you make Christ centered decisions.

Please understand, I'm not despising the Holy

Spirit as the perfect mentor in our spiritual path. He will never guide you wrong, right? Why would we need a real person to help us to grow in God? Did not Jesus say, *"for the Holy Spirit will teach you in that very hour what you ought to say."* in Luke 12:12? Yes, but I must to remind you that many times the Holy Spirit speaks through the mouths of His children, including your, especially when someone looks for help and hope. More than that, God allowed Paul to keep writing in his letters that he was a model to be followed as he followed Christ. He really said, *"..keep your eyes according to the example you have in us."*

Here again we might ask: "Was Paul a perfect person?". In 1 Timothy 1:15 he answered, " ... *Christ Jesus came into the world to save sinners, of whom I am the foremost."* So, Paul was not perfect, but he made disciples.

Then what would be the limit for a discipler to instruct someone who places himself as a disciple. Look what Paul said in 1 Corinthians 4:6: *"I have applied all these things to myself and Apollos for your benefit, brothers, that you may learn by us not to go beyond what is written, that none of you may be puffed up in favor of one against another."*

You need to get rid of this awkwardness you have in accepting a leader, a mentor, a voice in your life. I am not talking about following an unbiblical leader. A person who tries to dominate and create his own kingdom. When Paul said, "follow me" remember what he said before that: "I have applied all these things in my life. I have been practical with the gospel. I'm applying the scripture in my personal life."

Here is good advice: be aware of people who talk too much and who are so private that you never know their real life. Let's stop talking about things and actually put the scriptures into practice.

Never forget that some "spiritual" knowledge has the power to puff us up (1 Corinthians 8:1), but love builds up. What I love about discipleship is that it's a calling to love each other. It's not exclusively about knowledge and teaching. This is about real life, this is the real deal. To be a disciple is to be open to being loved and loving others as Christ loved us.

John 13:35 "By this all men will know that you are My disciples, if you love one another."

Pray now: *Lord Jesus thank You for the amazing opportunity of being Your disciple. Thank You for all of the trouble You went through, coming as a man to show me the way I should live. Most of all, I thank You for my leaders and pastors who are being used by You to make me Your disciple. I also pray that I can have the opportunity of being used in someone else's life, not only to speak once in their life, but to make real disciples for You as I am today. Amen!*

7
OVERCOMERS MAKE DISCIPLES

Matthew 28:19 *"Go therefore and make disciples of all nations, baptizing them in the name of the Father and of the Son and of the Holy Spirit..."*

There is no greater order than that. That's why it is called "The Great Commission." Jesus was kind to remind us that christianity is nonsense if we do not go and make disciples. Think a little more profoundly and you'll get it.

If you stand to make disciples, you will bring the responsibility on yourself. You will embrace the life of an overcomer, because now you are the practical and tangible example in others lives, but remember that you probably received from someone else.

I must say, there is a risk in discipleship. We place each other in such high expectations, that sometimes they frustrate us. There were betrayals in Jesus' ministry. There were conflicts in Jesus' discipleship group, but can I be sincere here: the crucial moment proves the true disciple.

Have you ever notice that God has no problem to showing the flaws and weaknesses of His heroes of faith? Take a look in the "hall of faith" of Hebrews 12 and go back to their stories in the old testament. You'll easily figure out that they may actually be the least likely heroes. Transparency is a powerful instrument by which we approach each other and create bonds and produce healing. The apostle James suggested *"confess your sins to one another and pray for one another, that you may be healed. The prayer of a righteous person has great power as it is working" (James 5:16)*. When I talk about transparency, I encourage it on both parts: disciple and discipler. It's kind of expected that a disciple will look for help and confess short comings. I want to encourage leaders, in a certain measure, to expose their limitations for their disciples. This breaks the barriers and also places ourselves at the same level of humanity; especially, because we all have the risk of becoming arrogant when we are placed as a leader.

Do not deceive yourself by thinking that you are not "so immature" and become puffed up. For Paul said he could have become boastful (2 Co. 12:7).

We are called to shepherd the precious flock of God. This means we must feed this flock (disciples) God's word and care for their needs. We are called to oversee not forgetting that in the end we're building up the church. 1 Peter 5:2 explains that we must do so willingly, and have fun doing it. I can say that my best friends and closest christian brothers are my disciples, my pastors, and my old leaders. There is an immense joy in surrounding yourself with people who really love God.

Peter continued his instruction, pointing out the most common spoiler in disciple-making: money. The apostle said that we should serve each other eagerly, not for shameful gain. How many great friendships and amazing leadership teams have been destroyed because of the "love of money" (1 Tim. 6.10). So please, do not turn this great relationship into a partnership of business, but let Jesus be the center.

As disciple makers, we are not called to be perfect. The goal is to be good examples to the flock. God entrusted His precious people into your influence. Souls were bought by His precious blood, therefore, do not try to stand and say: "This is my flock. This one is my disciple..." These are God's people, and He entrusted them to you. The point is to form the body of Jesus-- the Church. Real Church happens only when real discipleship takes place.

Paul really made many disciples. He was one of the greatest disciple makers ever. He tells us his secret in *1 Corinthians 15:10 "But by the grace of God I am what I am, and His grace toward me was not in vain. On the contrary, I worked harder than any of them, though it was not I, but the grace of God that is with me."* I know it sounds pretentious, but he actually said: "I worked harder than any of the other apostles." Wow! He just said he made more disciples than anybody else! How dare you Paul? Notice, that it was all by the grace of God!

We must understand that! Do not try discipleship without grace, otherwise a terrible patriarchal domination will start. I have seen this happening many times. Great church planting moments becoming a mere political exchange.

Everything starts with grace, and through grace we are what we are! Jesus, who is with us, is the only "founder and perfecter of our faith" (Heb. 12:2). Real grace should result in real discipleship. Paul said he was more fruitful than others because he had the revelation of grace. Paul was an in-the-field-soldier, because of grace. The understanding of the the gospel drives us to become aggressive disciple-makers! You never saw the apostle Paul traveling alone. He would always take one of his disciples with him. He understood that grace was released for him to live a sacrificial life of constant giving and teaching.

To close: I would like to bring up the concept of the three levels of a healthy discipleship. In the book of Acts we have three very important protagonists: Paul, Barnabas and Timothy. I want to use their roles in the book of acts to illustrate a healthy discipleship life-style.

Paul needs Timothy: Acts 16:1-3 says *"A disciple was there, named Timothy ... he was well spoken of by the brothers ... Paul wanted Timothy to accompany him, and he took him ..."*

Paul was a disciple maker. As soon as he met Timothy he perceived the willingness of the boy to become a disciple. Every real disciple-maker must have a good disciple to invest in. Do you have a real disciple in which you are investing your life into?

Timothy needs Paul: *1 Timothy 1:2 "To Timothy, my true child in the faith: Grace, mercy, and peace from God..."*

Every disciple has a discipler, a mentor. Timothy had his great opportunity to join the first mission-agency once he met Paul and he did not miss the chance to be discipled by the great apostle Paul. Timothy became a true spiritual son to Paul. This talks about true complicity and partnership with your leader and mentor. Who speaks into your life? Do you have a discipler or mentor whom you trust for guidance?

Paul needs Barnabas: *Acts 13:1 says "Set apart for me Barnabas and Saul (then called Paul) for the work to which I have called them."*

This is the friendship level in ministry. This is the brother whom you have on the same level of maturity and experience as you. These are the few people that walked alongside of you and shared trials and stories with you. With whom do you share jokes and past stories in ministry and serveing God? Do you have good friends who share dreams and the same heart for the Lord?

An overcomer walks in real discipleship, making disciples, being a disciple and walking with otherworldly disciples.

Pray now: *Lord, You are the greatest of all disciple makers. I want to follow You and respond to the great commission (Matthew 28:19-21). Your promise said You will be with me every single day of my life and today is no different. I will make a disciple for Christ. I pray for these lost friends that have not given their hearts to Christ yet. I pray You give me a chance to share Your plan of salvation and invite them to become a disciples. Today, I intercede for my discipler (say the name of your mentor, leader or pastor). I trust that You placed this brother/sister in my path to make me a disciple of Christ. Give this discipler the patience and endurance to continue to serve and share Your teachings .I pray in Jesus' name. Amen.*

8
OVERCOMERS TAKE UP THEIR CROSS

*Mark 8:34 "And calling the crowd to Him with His **disciples**, He said to them, "If anyone would come after Me, let him deny himself and take up his cross and follow Me."*

The call to overcome is the same as being called to be a disciple. The call of a disciple is a call to be a follower, and consequently, if anyone would walk with Jesus, he will have to deny himself and take up his cross. The cross is not about salvation; it is about conquering the kingdom.

The message of the cross deeply touched the apostles' lives. Disciples have a lifestyle that reflects the cross. We should preach about the cross and also live by the cross. An overcomer lives what he preaches. When an overcome speaks, he should speak of his own testimony.

If you want to prevail, you need to know not only of the Lord Jesus' substitutional death, but you must take the Lord Jesus' cross as your own cross in experience. We must be able to say, *"I am crucified with Christ" (Gal 2:20)* and, *"The world has been crucified to me and I to the world" (6:14)*.

Paul's meekness, endurance, infirmities, weeping, sufferings, and chains were all the manifestation of the life of the cross. He was one who lived by the cross and because of that he could preach the cross.

The world constantly criticizes us Christians for being those who do not practice what we preach. Yet, in reality, no one should ever preach what he does not practice! When we have spiritual reality, we become able to live out the gospel and also to beget many spiritual sons and daughters through the gospel. We will possess the life and power of the cross. As a result, we will reproduce this cross in the hearts of others.

There is a power that comes from a life that is crucified. Paul says in 2 Corinthians 4:12 "*So death is at work in us, but life in you.*" When "death operates in us" others will experience life. I have seen in some marriages that when one of the spouses decides to operate or experience death daily, the whole family enjoys life. Jesus challenges us every day to allow the cross to do a deeper work in our hearts so that others can gain life. Why do some brothers bear more fruits than others? It is because only those who have died can give others life. If one does not have the death of the cross in himself, others cannot gain the life of the cross. How difficult this is!

What does death mean here? Death here is not only a death to sin, oneself, and the world. Death here has a deeper significance. This is a death that generates life. It was the inspiration of generating life that led Jesus to the cross. We know that our Lord Jesus Christ did not die for His own sin, since He had no sin. On the contrary, His self-deliverance was the manifestation of His holiness. Jesus' crucifixion was entirely on behalf of others. Jesus died in obedience to God's will, so we could be saved. This is the meaning of this death.

Taking up our own cross is not for our own sake. We should be crucified to sin and the world, but it is for the sake of our obedience to the Lord as a picture of the love with which He once loved us. Thus, when you face opposition, whatever the circumstances you may be facing, you should decide to take up your cross for the sake of others. We put ourselves to death for the sake of the lost world.

We should allow the death of the Lord Jesus to work in us to the point that we truly have the experience of dying to ourselves and become sanctified. Furthermore, we should allow the Holy Spirit, through the cross, to do a deeper work in us so that we can live out the cross. We should not only have the death of the cross, but even more, we should have the life of the cross. When we have the death of the cross, we are dead to sin and the Adamic life and the old habits that controlled us in the past. When we have the life of the cross, we go one step further and take the cross as the very life in our daily living. This means that we manifest in our daily living the Spirit of the Lord Jesus as the Lamb, who suffered silently and who *"being reviled did not revile in return; suffering, He did not threaten but kept committing all to Him who judges righteously"* (1 Pet. 2:23).

This is a step further than being crucified to sin, oneself, and the world. May the cross become our lifestyle, thus we can be a living Christ in our family.

We are able to give others life when our life means being at the cross. We must not apply the cross in a passive way, but actively take the cross as our lifestyle, to terminate everything from the old Adam. Day by day apprehend the significance of the Lord's cross and at the same time, day by day, express the life of the Lord as the Lamb. As Paul boldly said *"always carrying in the body the death of Jesus, so that the life of Jesus may also be manifested in our bodies"* 2 Corinthians 4:10.

To be willing is to be *"always..delivered unto death for Jesus' sake that the life of Jesus may also be manifested in..mortal flesh"* (v. 11). The result of such deliverance is the same experience of the apostles, that when *"pressed on every side was not constricted; when was unable to find a way out did not feel utterly without a way out; when persecuted did not think was completely abandoned; when cast down could feel not destroyed"* (vv. 8-9). How could Paul handle such great stress in life and not despair? Because he allowed the death of the Lord Jesus to "operate" in him (v. 12). He experienced the death that operated as a "living death." It is the life that comes from death, the life of resurrection. That's why Paul was always willing to be delivered unto death for Jesus' sake. He was willing to endure ear-grating words, arrogant people, cruel p e r s e c u t i o n s, a n d u n r e a s o n a b l e misunderstandings, all for the Lord's sake. When we give ourselves to this level of deliverance we will be able to hold our hasty words and always express Christ.

To walk by the cross is to be able to have the power to ask the Father to send twelve legions of angels to the rescue and to change all circumstances, but choose not to do it. You would rather let the "living death" of Jesus (the life and spirit of the cross) work in you. You must realize that with the cross there is power, a power which enables you to suffer persecution and tribulations and in the end endure and stand firm. How deeply has the cross worked in your life? Are we ready, if necessary, to bear *about in the body the putting to death of Jesus?"* Are you able to say to the Lord that you are willing to die and not resist all suffering and opposing circumstances?

In the process of becoming a disciple, we tend to expect that the other part takes up the cross, but if we want others to learn the path of the cross, the cross must first take hold of us. It is only after the cross has been brought into our lives through the fiery sufferings and oppositions, that we can duplicate this cross in others' lives. In other words, the "life of the cross" is released only when we walk through the narrow way.

The Bible clearly tells us that we are ministers, not just for preaching, but for the manifestation of the life of the Lord Jesus, and we are to extend the life of the Lord Jesus from our body. We can only fan out His life when we live and decide to put on the death of Jesus everyday. Let us pour out life unto death for the Lord Jesus' sake. When we give up our reputation and our heart to the Lord, when we express the way of the Lamb of Golgotha in the midst of all sufferings, then we will see the stream of life flowing. I know we often like to take the shortcuts, and we should realize that there is no shortcut in manifesting the life of the Lord Jesus!

When the death of the Lord Jesus is able to work in us, we will be able to see the life of the Lord Jesus working in the disciples the Lord has giving us. When I say "life" here, I'm talking about the greek word "zoe," which in the original language, means the spiritual life, the highest life, the life from God. What we should desire, is that people who learn from us will gain the spiritual life of the Lord, the life that operates in the hearts and enables the disciple to reach his or her God-given purpose. This is not vain preaching, but when facing a hard hearted audience you will be able to flow streams of living water to them.

When we stand as overcomers, our preaching has to have this power that produces results of salvation and discipleship. We should not be satisfied when we do not see the results of transformation, repentance and encouragement when we share the word of God! In summary, one who does not live the cross, cannot expect to bear fruits as Paul, Peter, John, as overcomers...as Jesus.

Pray now: Christ Jesus, thank You for the cross and Your sacrifice made there, and thank You for showing me the way to trust God all the time and in the craziest circumstances. Through the Holy Spirit in me, help me to fight against my own will and do your perfect will. Help also my friends and family (mention someone's name) to understand what You conquered at the cross, and let more people make the decision to go down in the waters of baptism. Amen.

9
OVERCOMERS RECEIVE REWARDS

Matthew 25:19-21 "*Now after a long time the master of those servants came and settled accounts with them. And he who had received the five talents came forward, bringing five talents more, saying, 'Master, you delivered to me five talents; here, I have made five talents more.' His master said to him, 'Well done, good and faithful servant. You have been faithful over a little; I will set you over much. Enter into the joy of your master.'* "

God will come and ask for the gift He entrusted into our hands. It's not about our own gifts, our own abilities, our own money or our own potential... it's about what He gave to us, and because it belongs to Him, He can ask for accountability. Many brothers answer the same way: "Pastor, here is my talent back because I can't serve like this anymore... I'm feeling weak. I see myself as so unprepared. I'm incapable... I, I and I..."

They forget that it's not about them or what they have, but it's about what the Lord gave to them.

The faithful servant said so correctly: *"Master, you delivered to me... here it is what is yours God, but I'm not giving it back the way you gave it to me, I'm bringing it multiplied."* How did this servant figure out that the master expected this multiplication? Notice that the Master did not ask for any kind of work from the entrusted servants. James 4:17 explains saying *"So whoever knows the right thing to do and fails to do it, for him it is sin."* So, you and I should therefore hold firm to our calling and responsibilities that the Lord has entrusted us.

The talent in this parable was a great amount of money. I think money is the best factor to show our faithfulness. Usually, our money comes to our lives as a result of our own ability, our capacity to deal with our finances. Now, let's read again the criteria used by the Master who entrusted different amounts of money to his servants: Matthew 25:15 *"each according to his ability."*

I believe that God will consider our capability, but most importantly, everyone will receive at least one talent. No believer can say he is totally dispensable. The Master entrusted at least one talent to each servant. So stop excusing yourself by saying you have nothing to multiply, and be useful in God's kingdom! God is empowering you now with great potential and also responsibility. Isn't this wonderful? God gives us the talent, then He empowers us with His grace and because we stand faithfully, we'll get a reward in the day of judgement. I think this is awesome!

Maybe you're not used to this concept of being rewarded by God based on your faithfulness, because usually, we do not hear much about it. The truth is no one will be rewarded because he received a gift. Notice that everyone received a great gift, but the faithful ones were honored.

The gift and the reward both come from God, but there is a difference between the reward and the gift. We can also say there is a difference between the kingdom and eternal life. Many people think that the kingdom of heaven is the eternal life and vice versa, but eternal life is actually the gift. Anyone who decides by faith to receive it, will be granted eternal life, but being rewarded and honored in the kingdom of heaven is a matter of faithfulness. Please, understand that when the Bible is talking about the kingdom, it isn't talking about salvation, but about a reward. There are brothers who consider that when the Bible talks about the loss of the kingdom it is talking about the loss of eternal life, but there is no reference to believe in such a way.

A person may lose the kingdom of heaven, but not eternal life. Someone may lose the recompense: however, he will not lose the gift of salvation. What is the reward and what is the gift? We were saved because of the gift of God. He gave us eternal life freely by His grace. *Ephesians 2:8 "For by grace you have been saved through faith. And this is not your own doing; it is the gift of God."*

The reward speaks of how we relate to God after we have received eternal life. A christian receives salvation because of the work of the Lord Jesus. After receiving salvation, he must manifest the victory of Christ through the Holy Spirit in his day-to-day life to receive the reward. At the end of the race, the faithful servant will obtain the glorious heavenly reward of God. *2Timothy 4:6-8 " ...I have fought the good fight, I have finished the race, I have kept the faith. Henceforth there is laid up for me the crown of righteousness, which the Lord, the righteous judge, will award to me on that Day, and not only to me but also to all who have loved his appearing."*

Salvation is the first step on this path and the reward is the last. After salvation, you need to begin the race to receive future glory, a crown. God places His crown, glory and recompense before each one of us. If we are faithful, we will receive it.

You know that God never saves a person because of his merits, right? But also it is implied that He never rewards a person that does not have any merit. In order to receive salvation, we must come to God completely without merit. However, after receiving salvation, we must be faithful and strive to make disciples through His grace in order to receive the reward. (Matt. 28:19-20).

Many think that the great glory is the grace of salvation, and consequently, they become compromised and weak in their walk. Salvation separates the saved ones from the lost ones; faithfulness separates those saved, His children, into two groups as well: the overcomers and the defeated, the obedient from the disobedient. God will separate those that love the world from those that love the Kingdom.

Revelation 2: 23 "...I will give to each one of you according to your works." 1 Corinthians 3:14 " If the work that anyone has built on the foundation survives, he will receive a reward." These verses say that the Lord will honor those who have works and deeds. The reward depends on the work of the person. The Bible clearly distinguishes between salvation and reward. Do you understand that? As overcomers, we should never mistake salvation with reward, neither confuse faith and works. Without faith man cannot be saved, and without works a believer cannot receive the reward. God has a reward awaiting for each one of us, but to be a conquerer is a matter of endurance and faithfulness. Stand and put into practice, today, every teaching and revelation you once received. Pray right now that God creates an opportunity to share the gospel. Be a doer of the Word, not only a listener. Let your faith arise and produce many fruits. Be a disciple. Be an overcomer. So Jesus said to the Jews who had believed in Him, *John 8:31 "...If you abide in My word, you are truly My disciples."*

Pray now: *Jesus, You promise to reward those who overcome. I pray and stand this day responding to the call to become an overcomer. Grant me the chance to pray and minister in someone's life today. Lord, You are my great reward and gift. Thank You so much for Your grace upon my life, use me more.*

Today I pray for the LifeGroup Leaders of my church. Lord, grant them courage to preach Your message. Let them experience the provision that comes over every one who seeks Your kingdom (Matthews 6:33). I trust You to hear my prayer. In Jesus' name! Amen.

10

OVERCOMERS HONOR

1 Samuel 24:4-5 "Then David arose and stealthily cut off a corner of Saul's robe. And afterward David's heart struck him, because he had cut off a corner of Saul's robe."

During the establishment period of the kingdom of Israel, God officially established His authority on earth. When the Israelites entered Canaan, they asked God for a king, and God sent Samuel to anoint Saul as their first king (1 Sam. 10:1). Saul was chosen by God. God set him as the authority, that is, as His deputy authority. When he became king, Saul did not submit to the authority of God. He violated God's authority, by refusing to kill the king of Amalek and the best of the sheep and oxen. He rebelled against God and disobeyed His words; therefore, God set Saul aside and anointed David (1 Sam. 15—16). However, David was under Saul's authority. He was one of Saul's subjects and was even a soldier in Saul's camp.

Later, he even became Saul's son-in-law. Both of these men had the anointing upon them, but Saul often sought to kill David. There were two kings in Israel: one God had set aside, but still sat on the throne; and the other was chosen, but did not make it official. In this situation David was still trying to submit and honor his predecessor.

Saul chased David everywhere. There was a moment when Saul went into a cave to use it as a toilet, and that was where David and his followers were. David's followers suggested that he kill Saul, but David rejected this. He understood that suggestion as a temptation. David understood that to honor means not rebelling against authority.

What is crazy, is that David was already anointed by God. He could claim the throne, after all it was God who called him, but David decided to stand in the proper position with God's plan and will.

Maybe he would never have to tell anybody about how he would become king, for that was rightfully his position. What would have been wrong with David helping himself become king? Would it not have been a good way to help God accomplish His will? He chose not to act upon the natural response. He saw that if he had killed Saul, it would have been, in principle, rebellion against God's authority. The anointing of God was still upon Saul.

Maybe you ask, "Wasn't Saul rejected by God? How is it then, that he was still God's anointed?" Remember that God does not act as we do. *Romans 11:29 "For the gifts and the calling of God are irrevocable."*

Maybe David could have become king immediately, but David understood that God's will could be delayed or arrive early. Honor requires self denial. David would rather see the apparent delay in God's plan, than to become rebellious. As a result, he was eventually given God's authority. Honor shows the meekness for God's timing. David didn't want the kingship at the price of rebellion. The understanding of honor passes into the revelation of authority. To learn honor, you must see submission and authority as relevant.

People who want to lead need to find a leader to submit to. The useful man of God will always submit to authority. Submission is more important than results in our work in ministry. Even if David set the whole kingdom in order, this would avail nothing without being under God's authority.

When Saul preserved the best of the sheep and the oxen, and decided he would not destroy them, but rather saved them for an offering, he was actually under the principle of rebellion, even doing something apparently right and godly. The point is : outward religious offerings cannot cover up a rebellious heart.

If David wanted to, he could have easily killed Saul, and then he could have served the people of Israel right away, but David decided not to do this. He waited for God to work in the situation. He was submissive. When we are truly born again, we have this feeling as well. Our desire is only to please God and never hurt a brother or sister. That is why John said in 1 John 2:9 "*Whoever says he is in the light and hates his brother is still in darkness.*" We ought to be free from the spirit of rebellion and retaliation.

David had been chased by Saul many times, yet he still did not pay him back for his wrong doing. He considered Saul as a representative of the Lord, the anointed of Jehovah. Here is the lesson: submission to authority is not submission to a person. It is submission to the anointing upon that person, the anointing which was upon him when God set him as the authority.

David recognized the anointing on Saul. He acknowledged that Saul was God's anointed. Hence, he could only seek for his own escape. He could not put forth his hand to hurt Saul. We all know that Saul was disobedient to God's command and came to be rejected by God, but this was something between Saul and God. As for David, he submitted to God's anointed. This was David's responsibility before God.

David had the same chance to kill Saul twice. Look at 1 Samuel 26. A similar thing happened in the wilderness of Ziph. In the second temptation, Saul fell asleep, and David came into the place where he slept. Abishai wanted to kill Saul, but David forbade him. He swore and said, "*Who can stretch forth his hand against the Lord's anointed and be guiltless?*" This was the second time that David spared Saul. He only took Saul's spear and water jug (vv. 7-12). We also will have the chance to stand against our leaders, and some times even with good reason, but this is our test, not theirs.

David honored God's authority in the person of Saul, which is another reason he was called a man after God's heart. His kingdom has been preserved until now, for the Lord Jesus is a descendant of David. Only those who submit to authority, can themselves have authority. This is a serious matter. We must uproot rebellion from among us and learn the path of honor. In order to be an authority, there must first be honor and submission. This is crucial. Without honor, we have no way to prosper.

Let us have a heart ready to walk in the nobility of the ones who belong to the court of the King Jesus, David's heir. Let us also keep a heart full of honor and willingness to submit for the kingdom's sake.

Pray now: *Lord, I recognize Your authority and Your throne over my life. I confess that You alone are my King forevermore, and that You have chosen and appointed specific people to help me find Your purpose for me. Today, I want to honor these people and honor You through them. I also pray that my brothers and sisters (mention specific names) can also understand that they are not being lowered when they honor, actually they will be raised up by Your almighty hands, and receive honor from God when they honor the ones You have appointed. I want to pray for all the missionaries and those who have dedicated their lives to You, those who are not being recognized or honored properly all over the world. I pray that they can hold fast, waiting for the day that You will honor them before all nations for their sacrifices. Amen!*

11

OVERCOMERS SERVE
(By Calixto Said)

The overcomer serves more than all others.

Mark 9:35 (ESV)
*And He sat down and called the twelve. And He said to them, "If anyone would be first, he must be last of all and **servant of all**."*

Galatians 5:13 (ESV)
*For you were called to freedom, brothers. Only, do not use your freedom as an opportunity for the flesh, but **through love serve one another**.*

Serving other people sounds so against the American culture that some of you have already closed your hearts to learning this principle. If you read the verses above, you will see that God's idea is that we serve others as much as we can, according to Mark 9:35. Also, according to Galatians 5:13, we should use the freedom we have in Christ to serve more, with love.

So, since our God is very good, let me give you three awesome reasons to serve:

1. To be the first

Actually you can't really be "The First", because Jesus already is, and He conquered it by serving all. The work of the cross was enough to bless every single person in every corner of the Earth, and in every second of time. Jesus literally served all, and became the first in heaven.

As Christians, caring for our eternal lives more than just this temporary life, should be critical. Its reasonable to invest in a retirement plan, so one can live more comfortably the next 40 "ish" years. Likewise, it is very important to "invest" in the next millenniums of your life! To the world, it's non-sense, but for us, that's just how it is, after all, we are eternal.

2. You have the right to

It is impossible for non-believers to think about serving. Even though they think they are free, indeed they are not, and can't serve God voluntarily.

We as believers were set free by Jesus, our savior and redeemer, and now we have the "right" and the freedom to go against the worldly teachings, and serve as much as we can.

3. It is a great privilege

In Colossians 3:23 and Ephesians 6:7, we see that we should serve others as serving the Lord. So, even though in the sight of others we serve people, in our hearts we must be convinced that we are serving God and no one else. It is a privilege for few to serve God voluntarily, and the way God arranged it to happen is by serving our brothers and sisters.

The overcomer understands this privilege and the rewards of serving, so, don't waste your time thinking of what others are saying about you.

Serve more than all, for you are an overcomer.

Pray now: *Jesus, You served more than anyone. You are the Master, yet You washed the feet of the disciples. I ought to wash my brothers' feet as well (John 13:14). I'm ready to respond as Christ. I intercede today for the leaders in training in my church. God, I ask that You place in the heart of each of these leaders a readiness to always serve Your church. Raise them up as faithful members of Your body. Grant them perseverance and determination for the work of the ministry. In Jesus' name. Amen.*

12
OVERCOMERS MAKE THEIR FAMILY THRIVE

When the Word of God speaks about eternal life the individual is always the center point of the message. However, when it comes to salvation, God always uses the expression of our house, our family as the target listeners. We believe salvation is for us and for our home. Our faith is sustained by God's promises. The promises are where the blessings of God are. It is clear that the Bible promises salvation for our family.

When we talk about family, this includes couples and their children, so we should not fear seeing our children unsaved or lost, for the covenant of God extends to them. Therefore, pray earnestly for your kids and believe they will be saved. Do not be negligent. Pray and see the miracle of salvation happen.

When Paul talked with the jail chief in Acts 16:31 he exclaimed to the jailer, *"Believe in the Lord Jesus, and you will be saved, you and your household* ." We see that throughout the Bible salvation is extended to the family. With this promise in mind, I now dare you to also see your family as destined to be a family that thrives and overcomes. How can we do that?

Here are some practical examples. On the occasion of the flood, "Then the Lord said to Noah, 'Go into the ark, you and all your household, for I have seen that you are righteous before Me in this generation.'" Noah received the favor, but he brought his whole family. Notice that the Bible says that Noah was righteous, but nowhere will you find it saying anything about his children being as good and just as he was. Still Noah put everyone into the Ark. He knew salvation was for his sons and his wife. With this faith, he convinced all of them to come into God's plan. Today, we must believe God will honor our faith and bring our family to His purpose.

Another example was Abraham. He made his whole house be circumcised. Abraham followed the instruction of God and did not give an option to his children nor to his servants. (Genesis 17.12-13). God made a covenant with Abraham and the sign of this covenant was circumcision. The order was: circumcise every male of your household. Abraham obeyed thus the covenant of God, which was only made with Abraham, was extended to his whole house. Overcomers receive the promises and their requirements, and apply them to the whole family. In times of fasting, I always try to involve my kids at their own level in the same atmosphere of prayer and devotion. This is a way we can try to get our family involved with the things of God.

In Exodus 12, we learn that on the occasion of the last plague in Egypt, God commanded them to celebrate the Passover. Salvation, at that moment depended on eating a roasted lamb and passing its blood on the portals of the house where the whole family was gathered. Sometimes we feel that our family is at risk or in danger. Here is a principle: the only way that death can pass afar is if we keep the whole family together inside the house where the blood has been sprinkled. When we hold together faith in the Lamb of God, sacrificed for our sins, we will endure.

Overcomers also practice the priesthood in their houses. The Lord separated Aaron and his family to be priests. If we understand the principle that we are made priests through our salvation, we can also say that our whole family was also separated to be ministers wherever we go. Try to encourage your children and spouse to become this priesthood wherever they study or work (Js 6:17).

Obed-Edom (2 Samuel 6:11) is another good example of how the blessing of God is for the whole family. In God's plan the main target for the blessing is not the individual, but the family.

Every leader of a house can seek the blessing of salvation for the whole family, for this is the promise of God. Notice that this is not only salvation, but includes each of the blessings of God for us and for our home.

When Jesus paid Zacchaeus a visit, that rich and corrupt man got saved. In the joy of his redemption he said, "I will restore any damage my former life has produced." Luke 19:9 writes: "*And Jesus said to him, 'Today salvation **has come to this house**, since he also is a son of Abraham.'*" Notice again that the transformed life of one person released salvation for all the members of the family. Perhaps, because we live in an extremely individualistic society, we may not agree that salvation is for the family as a unit.

The Bible sustains that if I believe that God saved me, He will also save my entire family.

Cornelius (Acts 10), the first non-jew believer had the practice of praying and giving to the poor. The result of his personal godly life was that all of his house was blessed with Peter's visit. Look what Acts 10:2 says, "Cornelius was *a devout man who feared God with all his household, gave alms generously to the people, and prayed continually to God.*" The salvation of Cornelius is a tremendous demonstration of how God comes for the household and not only for the individual. These days, our prayer is to reach our families for God's glory. Enter into the house of your friends and invite the whole family to your next LifeGroup meeting. Be bold and believe that when someone is open to the gospel, all of his family follows in the blessing.

If salvation follows the whole family, then God is also calling all the member of your house to stand as overcomers. Do not be conformed with less than seeing your children as faithful disciples of Christ. Do not stop praying until you see your spouse responding to God as you are. Always believe that Jesus called you and your house to be overcomers.

Pray now: *Father You call us Your family and are determined to turn us into corespondents of Your glory and victory. God I stand with my family, determined to make my family thrive.*

Father grant me a chance to minister Your gospel to my relatives. Holy Spirit move in their hearts, bringing the conviction that I cannot. I believe You have placed me in this family for the fulfillment of Your purpose. I pray in the name of Jesus Christ. Today I pray for Your church as the family of God. Let every brother and sister of my church understand that we should all build up Your house. In Jesus' name. Amen.

13
OVERCOMERS DEFEAT THE WORLD

God is a triune God, the Father, the Son and the Holy Spirit. As the early apostles defined it in an ideal picture: The Father is God; the Son is God; and the Holy Spirit is God, but the Father is not the Son; the Son is not the Holy Spirit; the Holy Spirit is not the Father. Three persons are one perfect unit, one God in perfect harmony. Trinity is a beautiful mystery and no good illustration is sufficient to impeccably draw it.

As there is the Divine Trinity, there is also the evil trinity. We have the three entities that always counterattack our devotion to God. The devil is that wicked being that Jesus overcame in Matthew chapter 4 and Luke 4. Jesus used the Word of God to stand against Satan. The scriptures were the defense and weapon of attack used by Jesus to beat the tempter and accuser of our soul (Revelation 12:10). Jesus finally defeated him on the cross. Here is good advice: we can fight against our enemy with many strategies and words, but we definitely overcome him when we take up our cross (Matthew 16:24).

Secondly, we have the flesh. Galatians 5:17 says, *"This is the inner enemy that stands against the Spirit of God in our heart. For the desires of the flesh are against the Spirit, and the desires of the Spirit are against the flesh, for these are opposed to each other, to keep you from doing the things you want to do."* Our flesh needs to be disciplined and never trusted. We should never rely on our own knowledge. Proverbs 3:5 *"Trust in the Lord with all your heart, and do not lean on your own understanding."* The "flesh" speaks of this essence of ego and self righteousness that creates a false sense of capacity and arrogance.

Finally, we have the World. This last element of the trinity of evil is clearly against God. John says: *"Do not love the world or the things in the world. If anyone loves the world, the love of the Father is not in him."*(1 John 2:15). The "world" here is *kosmos,* which usually was used in the Bible to describe that which rules the unbelieving world. The Strong's dictionary says that *kosmos* is the same as world affairs, the aggregate of earthly things. You must agree that the world is the most subtle of the enemies. Perceiving and fighting against a culture or a mentality that seems to be the norm is hard because it seems you must constantly go against the flow.

Apostle James insists James 4:4 " ... *Do you not know that friendship with the world is enmity with God? Therefore whoever wishes to be a friend of the world makes himself an enemy of God."* The symbolism here is that of a person that spends time, confidence and resources with "a friend" that is clearly an enemy of God. You trust this friend, you walk and rely on this friend, consequently, you will despise God.

Overcomers, however, will love God more. They seek time, spend resources, talk and walk with their real Friend, which is God. If the saying *"…the enemy of my enemy is my friend"* thus true friendship and intimacy with God is also a result of resisting the world. The truth is that our culture, government, education, fashion, economy, etc… are all doomed. John affirms in 1 John 5:19 *"… the whole world lies in the power of the evil one."*

How can we overcome the world? How can we walk in victory against the *"kosmos"?* It's simple: Loving God and His kingdom more. You defeat the world when you rely on God more than the things of this earth, Matthew suggests *"seek first the kingdom of God and His righteousness, and all these (earthly) things will be added to you."* Matthew 6:33. We stand against the world by keeping our eyes on the rewards of heaven. Expecting and desiring "what God has prepared for those who love Him". The promise in 1 Corinthians 2:9 is *"what no eye has seen, nor ear heard, nor the heart of man imagined…"* I don't know if you get excited about this, but I dream of this other place while I am a sojourner in this world. Paul completes the idea in 1 Corinthians 15:19 saying *"if in this life only we have hoped in Christ, we are of all men most pitiable."*

When we love the things that God loves, we will place our heart in the right place to become real overcomers. Interestingly, the word *kosmos is* also used in the famous John 3:16 verse: John 3:16 *"For God so loved the world, that He gave His only Son, that whoever believes in Him should not perish, but have eternal life."* The question now is, how can we hate the things of the world and at the same time love the world as God loves? Colossians 1:13 explains: *" He has delivered us from the domain of darkness and transferred us to the kingdom of His beloved Son."* We do not belong to the world anymore. Now, we have the responsibility to shine the light we once received to this lost world, and when we do this, we express that we truly love God.

Peter encourages us saying: 1 Peter 2:9 *"But you are a chosen race, a royal priesthood, a holy nation, a people for His own possession, that you may proclaim the excellencies of Him who called you out of darkness into His marvelous light."* This holy nation is out of the world, out of the mindset and the rules of this world. This holy nation is the Church, which was chosen to proclaim the love, patience, goodness and the mercy of God to the world. We are this nation of overcomers.

Pray now: *Lord God, I want to love You more. I understand that I can only love You because You loved us first (1 John 4:19) I give my heart to You. I love You Jesus! Help me to see the world as You see it. I want to keep my eyes constantly on You. Deliver me from the mindset of this world. I set my mind on the things of heaven not on the things of the earth (Colossians 3:2). I have this passion in my heart to see the nations bow and all the world know You. So for the sake of the lost world, burn like a fire in my heart. I pray for everyone in my (give name of the place you spend most of your time: school, work place, etc.) to recognize Your salvation. I also pray for evangelism to become the culture of my church. That our way of life always includes a fervor to preach and share Your gospel. Amen Lord!*

14
OVERCOMERS ENJOY GENEROSITY

The Bible talks a lot about money. Matthew 6:24 - "*No one can serve two masters, for either he will hate the one and love the other, or he will be devoted to the one and despise the other. You cannot serve God and money.*" Jesus did not give the option to see money as something neutral or a small thing in our spirituality. Actually, He said that the worship and love we have for God should be exclusive and cannot have any impediment, but the only thing that can remain between God and our heart is money, so money says a lot about our spirituality.

It is understandable that this subject bothers many people, because it is through our money that we express our spiritual reality, and the truth is that many brothers and sisters just want to be occasional followers of Jesus instead of committed disciples that walk in the pattern of overcomers. God is calling you to step into a new degree of trust and to experience generosity to its fullest.

Undoubtedly, money can become a major problem between what God has placed in your heart and the actual fulfillment of it. It is time to learn how overcomers deal with this barrier that comes against the vision God has put in their heart. The right answer is generosity. Before we go deeper into this subject, I want you to have the willingness to try and experience the supernatural provision and intervention in your life as soon as you finish this chapter. Please, do not read about "How God wants to prosper you and open the gates of heaven into your finances" if you're not ready to first give and be generous.

Jesus once said *"If then you have not been faithful in unrighteous wealth, who will entrust to you the true riches?"* (Luke 16:11). It is clear that faithfulness is the first practical aspect. It's not about the amount, but the constant faithful practice of giving. I know brothers and sisters who give here and there, but they do not maintain a constant practice of generosity; therefore, they have a faint experience of prosperity. God wants to entrust "true riches" to us, but the criteria is clear: faithfulness.

We must learn how amazing it is to give. There was a Youtube video about a father recording his daughter in a restaurant. As they ate, looking out the window, the daughter saw a homeless man laying on a public bench. After asking her father why that man was laying there on the street all alone, he said, "He is a poor guy that does not have anything to eat or even a place to sleep." "Do you think we can help him?" the girl asks without any hesitation. The father gives her an affirmative nod and allows her to bring this poor man some food. Her father with the camera, records this act. At the end of this short beautiful video, the girl walks back and her father asks,

"How do you feel, daughter?". Joyfully the little girl replies, "I liked it!". Acts 20:35 is true when it affirms *"It is more blessed to give than to receive."* If you have never experienced the joy and blessing of giving, you won't know what we're talking about.

We are so used to consumerism that we do not believe that giving and acting freely in generosity is actually a blessing. The truth is that it is a blessing! A heart of giving is great proof of having a real experience with Jesus. If you have Jesus, you will have a heart of giving. Here is a example: Luke 19:8-10 *"And Zacchaeus stood and said to the Lord, 'Behold, Lord, half of my goods I give to the poor. And if I have defrauded anyone of anything, I will restore it fourfold.' And Jesus said to him, 'Today salvation has come to this house, since he also is a son of Abraham. For the Son of Man came to seek and to save the lost.'"* That fraudulent and greedy man received Jesus in his house and as a consequential reaction, he decided to give. Giving is always better than receiving.

We must learn to see money as a servant and not as a lord in our decisions. Many brothers and sisters are slaves of money. Every decision that they make is based on whether or not they have enough money. Here's the thing, our only lord, should be God. He should be the director of our decisions, the guider of our lives, but since we have the wrong perspective of money, it decides: how or where we should live, how many children we should have, which career or profession we should take, and on, and on...   Let the Lord deliver us from this relationship with money. Trust me, the method He will use is generosity. When we learn that money was entrusted to us, we will have a different point of view and use it for the right purpose, which is to bless the kingdom of God on Earth.

The overcomer walks in generosity because he understands that he is blessed with all treasures and blessings in the heavenly places. Ephesians 1:3 says that we are *"blessed... in Christ with every spiritual blessing in the heavenly places"*. Jesus taught us to pray *"Your kingdom come, Your will be done, on earth as it is in heaven."* (Matthew 6:10). The will of God is that all of the blessings He promised us and that are awaiting for us in the heavenly places, come to us now. I know many brothers and sisters who pray earnestly about their finances, but it seems that nothing changes. Why? Because the practical part of the prayer is not being obeyed: GENEROSITY. Remember you are in a position to be blessed, but the experience is only unlocked when we act by faith, practicing true generosity.

There is a church that placed a "90 Day Giving Challenge." When I saw this for the first time, I asked myself if this would not be a carnal way to bargain with God, but you know what, God lets Himself be tested in this matter. It appears that this is the only subject that God allows Himself to be tested. Look at Malachi 3:10 *"Bring the full tithe into the storehouse, that there may be food in my house. And thereby **put Me to the test**, says the LORD of hosts, if I will not open the windows of heaven for you and pour down for you a blessing until there is no more need."* You have probably heard a lot of testimonies of supernatural intervention in other people's lives after giving to God... but now is your moment. The church I mentioned above wrote on their website the following: "... we believe giving blesses God and that's why we want to be a church that is full of cheerful givers! Tithing not only helps ministries in our city and around the world to happen; it also brings you closer to God. We believe so strongly in this, in fact, that if you're willing to step out in faith and give the biblical definition of a tithe—10% of your income—for three straight months, and still don't believe God has been true to His promises, we will refund your tithe in full."

Overcomers dare to walk in faithfulness-- in generosity. They experience prosperity and abundance because they have tested the goodness of God and have learned that to give is better than to receive. Overcomers do not put their treasures on this earth. They do not hope in Christ, expecting the results only from the things of this life, but they understand that an eternal reward is awaiting for them. (1 Corinthians 15:19)

Pray now: *God, You are my only and absolute Lord. Nothing and no one has a higher place in my heart than You. Thank You for Your radical generosity in giving Your only begotten Son as a sacrifice for my salvation. I decide today to stand in generosity and faithfulness. I want to grow in this attitude. Please, God, enlarge my heart! (Psalm 119:32).*

I also pray for the resources of my local church. I ask for supernatural provision toward my community. I believe no eye has seen, no ear has heard, and no mind has imagined what You, God, have prepared for me! I love You. (1 Corinthians 2:9). Amen!

15
OVERCOMERS EVANGELIZE

When we started the church in Fort Myers, the main concern was how to establish a church with doors open to immigrants and at the same time American people. Southwest Florida is extremely diverse with cultural heritages from all around the world: central north USA, Germany, Latin America and the Caribbeans. How could we, Brazilian missionaries, plant a church with the possibility of embracing all of these cultures at once? We won't! We did not have the resources, in every sense of the word: financially, volunteers, and mainly evangelists.

We were a group of 12 people and God was sending the volunteers. So we started to try all that we had learn in the past. Few things worked the way they did in our headquarters in Brazil, but the principle that took The Vine Movement from one church in the central part of Brazil to more than 1300 churches around the world in only

20 years, was to remain: bold and aggressive evangelism.

God has shown us that the main reason for the existence of the church is to bring people from darkness into the light. 1 Peter 2:9 *"But you are a chosen race, a royal priesthood, a holy nation, a people for His own possession, that you may proclaim the excellencies of Him who called you out of darkness into His marvelous light."* We must be the proclaimers of all the attributes of God. You may ask if there is any help for that, because you don't want to feel awkward talking and sharing about a God that does not show up to prove Himself in case someone questions you. Romans 1:20 makes it clear that God has already proven Himself: *"For His invisible attributes, namely, His eternal power and divine nature, have been clearly perceived, ever since the creation of the world, in the things that have been made. So (the world and the unbelievers) are without excuse."* We are here only to "proclaim His excellence".

So if you are afraid that maybe evangelism won't work because people have a hard time seeing God in our post modern time, or because science has proven some new theory about the beginning of the universe, or your teacher insists that every spiritual experience is a matter of a psychological reaction... don't worry, God has already demonstrated Himself. We are only a "voice of one crying out in the wilderness..." We are a pointing sign. We do not convince, change the mind of, or force anyone, but God has called us to proclaim Jesus, and once the word meets the Spirit a new creation can happen. Remember how God created the "first" creation? *"Spirit of God was hovering over the face of the waters. And God said, 'Let there be light,' and there was light."* Genesis 1:2-3. It has always been like that. When the word meets the Spirit, revolution happens. Creation comes into existence and salvation is revealed.

Some brothers and sisters have failed in evangelism because they don't understand that transformation follows salvation. So, some devout brothers and sisters expect that for a person to be saved, first he or she must be transformed. It is because of mistakes like these, that we have many people "waiting" for their moment to give their lives to Jesus, since right now, they are not "right enough" to take the step of faith in Jesus... This legalist perspective holds back many potential evangelistic opportunities, so instead of worrying about clothing style, tattoos or what kind of food the person eats, the overcomer sees that if a person has stopped to listen, what matters is their openness. Romans 14:17 says : "*for the kingdom of God is not eating and drinking, but righteousness and peace and joy in the Holy Ghost.*"

Salvation comes by faith in Jesus. Faith comes through the preaching of the word of God (Romans 10.17). Here resides our duty: preach the word. We do not need to explain everything. We do not need to know all doctrines, but we need to preach. The word of God will do the work. My recent morning prayers have included the request for God to open my eyes to all the chances I'll have during the day to proclaim His word, and bring faith for salvation to everybody around me.

2 Timothy 4:2 exhorts us, "*...preach the word; be ready in season and out of season...*" Another translation for the word 'kēryssō' (preach) in this text is the word 'publish'. While I'm writing this book, I don't really know what you are thinking about my English, or the specific words I have

chosen in writing these phrases. I can't control what you feel or how you react to my "published" words, but my burden and passion is to obey God and proclaim His message. In the end, I have no authority over what will happen inside of you. Evangelism is the same. We "publish" the word of God and let the Holy Spirit work with this raw material of faith and bring salvation to each listener.

I truly believe there is not a more efficient and powerful strategy to evangelizing a person than small groups. People are tired of listening to theories and doctrines. They want to check out the reality of Jesus. They need to see His power working in real life. The best display of this is in the environment of a small group. Usually people are more open to an invitation to a friend's house than to a church building, so, dare to simply invite and let the surrounding of a great cloud of witnesses (Hebrews 12:1) do the rest. Let us believe that our testimonies will be sufficient to display Christ and the "*immeasurable greatness of His power toward us who believe, according to the working of His great might*" (Ephesians 1:19).

My 7 year old son is extremely sincere. He is in that phase in which he will comment on what he sees. So if he sees a bald man, I need to be prepared for the inevitable embarrassment of him pointing and describing what everyone has tried to be discreet about. We have had moments like these in the church, in restaurants, and so many other places. Obviously I always explain to him the need to be more polite and respectful with his comments, but usually he asked "But what did I say that was wrong? Is he not fat? Is he not bald?" And I always respond the same way "Son, remember that Jesus came in grace and truth (John 1:17), not only in truth." There are brothers that are ready to expose the failures and all the wrong doings of the lost person he is trying to evangelize. If you are speaking the truth, but without grace, in the end it will not bring Jesus to that person.

Today is an excellent day to start practicing this. You can boldly come to a person and explain the truth, their sinful condition and eternal condemnation, but never forget to soak these truthful words in the sweetness of grace. I love knowing that the harvest is plentiful (Matthew 9:35-38). Jesus said that the problem is not the hardness of the unbelievers, but the lack of laborers. We need more evangelists who will dare to evangelize and share the gospel whenever the situation allows.

Pray now: *Father God, I pray for this lost world that is still blind and under the influence of evil spirits that work in their minds and hearts, holding them in this stubbornness (Ephesians 2:2). Jesus, You made me a light in this dark world (Matthew 5:13) and there is no darkness that prevails Your brightness in me. I pray for evangelists and laborers in the plentiful harvest before me. I'm open to be the answer of this prayer. Help me, God, to perceive the opportunities You are creating around me for evangelism. I also pray for the next outreach event in my church. Let it be powerful and glorious, full of anointing and salvation. In Jesus' name. Amen.*

16
OVERCOMERS DON'T WASTE GRACE
(By Calixto Said)

2 Corinthians 6:1-2 " Working together with Him, then, we appeal to you not to receive the grace of God in vain. For He says, 'In a favorable time I listened to you,
and in a day of salvation I have helped you.'
Behold, now is the favorable time; behold, now is the day of salvation."

The grace of God is certainly the most precious thing the overcomer has access to. Actually, according to Titus 2:11, grace was made available to all people, and all who have access to something can become wasteful of it. If grace is available to someone that is rejecting it, it is being wasted. Everything that God did for those who are rejecting Him, is being made a waste by their rejection.

If grace is available to the Christians so they

do not have to worry about anything else except the expansion of the Kingdom, and they are still living under the law, worrying about pleasing God and conquering better things for themselves, grace is being wasted!

My next statement will probably be one of the strongest statements I will ever make in my life: Overcomers are the Christians who are using more grace than they are wasting.

Once I went with pastor Raphael to visit a brother in jail. He was there for driving once again without a driver's license, the number of times of which I do not know. What made things worse for him was that he had the right to have a driver's license. Everything was arranged for him to get a driver's license, but instead of going to the local DMV and paying 70-ish dollars to get his license, he had paid more than, THOUSANDS of dollars in bail bonds. A humongous price was paid at the cross, where Jesus conquered for us the right to receive all blessings (*Ephesians 1:3*), but instead of receiving them, we waste them and spend our lives chasing blessings we already have the right to receive! Doesn't that seem like a dog chasing its own tail? Isn't it a complete waste of time and everything else?

You probably have a good idea of how much Jesus suffered at the cross. All the physical and psychological pain, not to mention the weight of taking all of our sins. What if it was all for nothing? What if people just decide to ignore it and not use any of the benefits conquered with that sacrifice? All the pain and suffering becomes vain and useless, a waste!

Overcomers don't waste grace. They receive and use everything that was conquered at the cross, making the sacrifice of Jesus more and more valuable, multiplying its benefits in the lives of others who are being saved.

Pray now: *God, I have received grace for salvation and for the enjoyment of Your life. I decide today to use this powerful grace toward Your church. I ask that You give me the chance to minister this grace to my colleagues and friends. I want to be this channel of love and salvation.*
Today, I intercede for the hosts of the LifeGroups in my church. Father grant them a heart of hospitality (1 Peter 4:9), that each host and house that receives a LifeGroup can be prosperous and encouraged to persevere in the servitude of Christ. I ask in Jesus' name, Amen.

17
OVERCOMERS ARE PRIESTS

We have no doubt about our calling as a church. The Idea is to not play on positivism or try to psychologically inspire people with our mission's statement:

"Our mission is to build up a church of overcomers in which each member is a priest and each home is an extension of the church in order that we win over our generation for Christ through Life groups." We are being called to be ministers, act as priests and have the posture of leader. When 1 Peter 2:9 says we are " *a chosen race, a royal priesthood, a holy nation, a people for His own possession*" the idea is that we will stand, not only as occasional evangelists, but as constant ministers of God's grace.

A good definition for a "priest" would be a person that has the role of bringing the presence of God to the people, and also leading the presence of the people to God. You know that every professional or worker has a duty or a responsibility. When you hire a professional you expect that person to carry out their job with excellency. An incompetent doctor is one that doesn't know how to diagnose diseases and has no prognosis of a cure. An incompetent teacher is one that complicates   learning. So an incompetent priest poorly handles the presence.

In our church we challenge you to be a priest, which means   you can't fail dealing with the presence. To check and see if you are executing properly your role as a priest, see if there are people coming to you asking for prayer. Also, take an examining look at your Facebook and see if you have prayer requests on your page or only filtered selfie photos showing what you ate this morning. And please, don't feel accused in case you have realized you are not being a good priest. God wants to make you a better priest, even as you read this chapter.

Some faithful brothers and sisters fail to exercise their priesthood because they don't recognize the basis for this calling. They think that it is a matter of religious performance or legalism.   Revelation 1:5-6 is clear on the right basis for our ministry. It says that because Jesus *"loves us and has freed us from our sins by His blood"* He decided to make *"us a kingdom, priests to His God and Father"*.   The intention is to deliver all *"glory and dominion"* to Him *"forever and ever." It* is so crucial that we deeply ponder this.

Jesus' love for us enables us to show love toward others. If you do not "get" that He loves you, it will be really hard to be a faithful priest. The Amplified version of 1 John 4:19 says *"We, though, are going to love—love and be loved. First we were loved, now we love. He loved us first."*

What about our flaws and sins? They have a big weight on our work as the priesthood. No one under condemnation is able to be a strong priest. Is there any solution for our faults? Yes, there is, and it is not about your legalism, but it is about trusting in grace. God did not plan for your life to be a constant fight with temptation. Romans 6:14 says "*For sin will have no dominion over you, since you are not under law but under grace.*" So let's see if you got it: first He loved us, then He empowered us, now He makes us a kingdom of priests.

Now, if a doctor needs a medical office or a hospital to work; if a teacher needs a classroom to teach; a priest needs a temple to minister. For many, church is nothing more than a concrete building. Some go to the point of having reverence for the physical building and even call it the "house of God'". "*However, the Most High does not dwell in houses made by hands…*" says Acts 7:48. There are others that say they are going to the church, when actually they are referring to the church building. Is this building the temple, the "holy" place of God's presence? No! 1 Corinthians 6:19 says "*Or do you not know that your body is a temple of the Holy Spirit within you, whom you have from God?*" Therefore, your body is the place of ministry.

How does this works in a practical sense? You determine where the temple goes. Wherever you go, the temple goes with you. This is better than any portable electronic device ever invented! With smartphones, we have almost a complete computer in our pockets, but with your body, you have the complete temple of God within you! I think this is amazing. You can be a priest with boldness. You can enter and handle the presence, because you are the temple of God's presence. 1

Peter 2:5 illustrates this saying that we are *"like living stones"*. Peter affirms that we *"are being built up as a spiritual house"*. The goal is that we become *"a holy priesthood, to offer spiritual sacrifices, acceptable to God through Jesus Christ"*. Our own lives are now these *spiritual sacrifices*. So remember buildings are not sacred. We are the sacred ones where God abides.

We are called to serve people. We are called to serve the church. We should also serve the unbelievers, but above all, we minister to God. Forget about others' opinions and concepts. Do it for God. This kind of heart understands that commitment is not to please anybody else but God alone. A young sister expressed what I mean here when she said she is not going to date her boyfriend, but will have courtship standards. I asked why and she answered "I'm committing my relationship not to me nor to my boyfriend, but to God."

Paul teaches us how to be an effective priest. In Romans 1:9 he says *"For God is my witness, whom I serve with my spirit in the gospel of His Son, that without ceasing I mention you always in my prayers..."*. Overcomers are spiritual priests. It's not a matter of an ethical life or outward religion, but it's about the ministry of the presence. It's a matter of a life in the Spirit.

A priest knows how to flow in God's presence, in his spirit, until he becomes a channel to others. The priest knows the path of true worship and praise. John 4:24 reminds us when it affirms, *"God is spirit, and those who worship (walk with) Him must worship (have a life) in spirit and truth"*.

I pray that you may have the revelation that first God wants you to Himself. He longs for your presence in His presence. When His presence becomes a priority to us, then we will be overcomers. Our prayers will be answered and our words will be sealed with the Holy Spirit. Men like Samuel and Daniel were   used in power and authority because of their daily experiences with the presence. Daniel used to pray three times a day. By the end of his life he was known as the "servant of the living God" (Daniel 6:20). Samuel had the authority in his words, as speaking God's own words. 1 Samuel 3:19 affirms "the *Lord was with him and let none of his words fall to the ground*." I want this authoritative weight in my words, I want this kind of recognition on my life.

People will recognize the presence in your life. This is the call for priests. This is the call for the overcomers. The truth is that without an experience with the presence, without the real role of priesthood, our fruits will always be fake, fragile, and weak. Our words have no consistency, and our preaching has no effect.

Finally as priests we should serve Him with joy and satisfaction. John Piper puts it this way by saying "God is most glorified in us when we are most satisfied in Him." Which seems similar to what Psalm 16:11 affirms "...*in Your presence is fullness of joy, at Your right hand there are pleasures forevermore*." You must have that experience. Only the priests can truly enjoy such pleasure and delight. How about trying it now?

Pray now: *Jesus, Your sweet presence is the most elevated experience I can ever have. If there is anything I consider greater than being with You, it's because I have never actually entered into Your chambers of love... But I want this experience today. I want Your presence more than anything else. You are my life, my hope and my peace.*

Holy Spirit, I pray for the kids in my church. I pray these little children can indeed experience

Your love today. This is my prayer, Father! Amen.

18

OVERCOMERS LEAD

Have you ever felt that nagging, uncomfortable feeling that something must be done in your neighborhood or community? The feeling that you have to stand for Christ and God's kingdom no matter what? I remember the day I watched the movie "City of God" for the first time. The movie shows the story of the beginning of a Brazilian slum in Rio de Janeiro, between the end of the 1960s and the beginning of the 1980s. The drama is extremely realistic with all of the violence and perversion that a human being can have in a state of extreme poverty. I arrived home from the movie theater and could not sleep because of the sense of responsibility, after all that was my country, my nation. I was 17, and the only thing I could do was cry and pray for God to change that scenario in my nation. That was the day the Lord confirmed my calling as a pastor and pushed me even more in my leadership role with my teenagers' LifeGroup.

Have you ever felt something similar? It's because God is calling you to lead a LifeGroup. Do not quench the fire. Let it burn stronger. Do not flee from this pressing on the heart. Let it become a power inside of you. God is calling you to stand in your family, school or community to be a leader that will make changes for God's Kingdom.

It is this pressing that will drive you to attend barbecues, and hang outs at night, or to watch football games at the clubhouse. This calling will cause you to reach your neighbors, but remember that the convincing is not supposed to be on your shoulders. Do not assume responsibility that only God can take! Overcomers lead with the right pressure and burden in their hearts. They have the desire to show Jesus, period. Keep only the right passion, not the tiredness and disheartening. Be on fire but not "burned out".

Overcomers lead with the right responsibility. They make realistic goals, not vague and unattainable ones. They have a purpose to which people will be unalterably committed. They work to achieve the main purpose with the whole group, not the desires that change from one person to another. Do not confuse desires with goals. Our desire should be to see conversions in our neighborhood and to create a sense of community, but only God can make this happen. There are other roles that are about making it happen. For example, you invite your neighbor to play sports; invite your colleague over to your house for a special event (dessert, etc.); talk with a friend; encourage the members of the Lifegroup to begin the maturity track. Mainly, you can make your group come to multiplication.

Joel Comiskey says "Many leaders experience tension when thinking about this topic. A major cause of this tension is making unrealistic, vague goals based on lofty desires, rather than bite-size, feasible goals based on what can actually be done".

Overcomers do not resign even with the pressures and the problems of learning. Yes, we can become burnt-out. You must understand that leadership can have some traps, but God always gives us the way out. Learn to be a facilitator, the one who orchestrates the work for the whole group to carry out. The team should do the work with you, the leader. Everyone should participate!

An efficient leader prepares and facilitates the life of the weekly meeting. So the leader is the first to personally reach his lost friends for Christ. They meet with everyone in the group as often as possible and disciple them into strong believers. The idea is that everyone will want to get involved. A leader has a team, so learn to delegate all the various parts of your weekly meetings. Ask someone in the group to be in charge of meeting refreshments, prayer, worship and the ministry time. Every host can also be given the responsibility to plan and hold one fun event in the next three months to connect their unbelieving friends to the group.

An overcomer leader knows how to involve others and forces himself to delegate responsibility. In this way the group will become an exciting place of ministry and growth. Stop thinking that everything depends on you. The Psalmist wrote, "*Unless the Lord builds the house, its builders labor in vain. Unless the Lord watches over the city, the watchmen stand guard in vain*" (Psalm 127:1). Paul the apostle always had a team manner of working his leadership. He said "*I planted the seed, Apollos watered it, but God made it grow. So neither he who plants nor he who waters is anything, but only God, who makes things grow*" (1 Corinthians 3:6-7). Let us learn how to balance our leadership and influence with trust and reliance on God's work.

Overcomer leaders are not necessarily talented, gifted, or outgoing, but they do have one thing in common: they're persistent. They don't give up! They don't mind asking their members to invite someone to the group each week. You could compare what I'm saying to sowing and reaping. If you sow sparingly, you'll reap sparingly. If you sow bountifully, you'll reap bountifully. God hears every prayer you make, and He desires that you persist until the end. At times you'll want to give up; don't. God is hearing your prayers and is pleased with them. In His time the answer will come — quickly. Remember the Scripture Proverbs 14:23: *"All hard work brings a profit, but mere talk leads only to poverty."* Your diligence will lead to success if you keep on pressing on. God's blessing is right around the corner.

Overcomers understand the challenge in leadership, but they do not fear it. Even being hard once in an while, they don't try to do the work that belongs to God. They carry the easy yoke of Christ (Matthew 11:30), that's why they thrive.

Pray now: *Lord Jesus, You called me as Your servant and representative. I recognize my limitations, but all of them are only to bring glory and exaltation to You, that Your power might work through me. Help me today to be a better leader and stir my brother and sister's hearts to desire leadership. Today, I pray especially for my leaders in the church (pastors, disciplers, supervisors, LifeGroup leaders...) Let them continue be the voice of inspiration and persistence in my life. In Jesus name, amen.*

19
OVERCOMERS BUILD UP THE CHURCH

Matthew 16:18 " *And I tell you, you are Peter, and on this rock I will build my church, and the gates of hell shall not prevail against it.* "

Leaving the controversial aspects of this passage aside, (Was Peter or wasn't he the first pope? Is Peter or Peter's affirmation the rock?) we will focus on the "build my church" statement. God's first plan is to have a people in His likeness to express His character on Earth so, "*the earth can be filled with the knowledge of the glory of the LORD as the waters cover the sea.*" (Habakkuk 2:14). God planned to have you as a part of the greatest project ever designed. God called you to be a part of His church, His 'ekklesia'.

This greek word was used to represent a very special group of people in Rome at that time. They were a small sample of the Roman Empire. Usually the 'ekklesia' was formed of highly qualified Roman citizens, like doctors, philosophers and lawyers. This group was sent on a "mission" to a certain barbarian village   to display the benefits of being a Roman Citizen. Jesus used this symbol to express His idea of the church.

It's clear that the most important element of the church should be Jesus Himself. He said "*I will build my church*". That's already great news. Jesus will make it happen anyways, but it seems that He selected a certain building material for the work: "rocks". The concept is beautiful, but sounds impractical. Who is able to edify a building using only rocks? They have different shapes. Rocks come from erosion and were produced over time, and that's an excellent picture of what Jesus intended to say.

His "elite squad", His special selected ones, His church will be composed of the imperfect and the unlikely ones. While the Romans looked for the most qualified ones, Jesus chose rough rocks to build His Church. These are you and me. What I love in this picture is what Peter then wrote about the quality of these rocks. He said in 1 Peter 2:5 "*you yourselves like living stones are being built up as a spiritual house.*" So we have the constructors and the building material.

We are cooperators in this edification. Paul reminds us in 1 Corinthians 3:9 "*For we are God's fellow workers. You are God's field, God's building.*" God chose us in His sovereign grace for the praise of His Glory. Overcomers understand that they have a major role in God's ultimate project on Earth. They remain firm regardless of the threats of hell. In the end they believe that the gates of hell will not prevail, and the church will stand even with all the flaws and imperfections of these "living stones".

Jesus called us to build His church. This is also

a calling of high responsibility, because it is His church, His flock, His precious people. These are souls bought with the highest price. Jeremiah 48:10 *"Cursed is he who does the work of the Lord with slackness ..."* Some versions say deceitfully or negligently. The Message version says " *Sloppy work in God's name is cursed, and cursed is all halfhearted use of the sword."* I know the consequences of lukewarmness in serving Jesus' church sounds tough, but if you sincerely consider the price paid, and the love Christ has for His bride, you won't play around with this task.

Some brothers and sisters never commit their potential and talent to the church because they see the local church as the pastor's enterprise or a human project. I know there are some greedy ministers who use their messages for personal promotion,   but this cannot be used as an excuse to not serve God in a faithful and biblical local church. People that don't have the right view of the church always stumble at certain moments in their dedication because they are not perceiving that it is God's idea that is at stake here. They are dealing with God's main passion, His church. Stand today for your church. Call your pastor or leader and say you'll step up to a new level of devotion.

Pray now: *Lord Jesus, You gave it all for Your church. You are so passionate for Your bride. Give me the same burden and commitment toward my local church. I have received all these talents and gifts for the sake of Your purpose. I pray today for the the influence of my church in my community. You connected me to these beloved brothers and sister and I won't give up regardless of their differences and apparent flaws.In your name we pray. Amen!*

20
OVERCOMERS ENJOY GRACE

Genesis 1:28 (ESV) "*And God blessed them...*"

Notice that even before the order to multiply God blessed Adam and Eve. God released the blessings before any achievement or success from Adam. They had done nothing to this point, the blessing was from God alone, and then came the challenge "... *God said to them, 'Be fruitful and multiply and fill the earth and subdue it, and have dominion*'". God always gives first, and once you are blessed, once you have the promises, now you can stand and lead, be blessed by grace and be used by God. Grace is not a conditional of merit, it is free. I dare say: even if we do not respond to the second step of leadership the blessing will continue to be upon us.

God had no guarantee that Adam would respond to the challenge: "*be fruitful and multiply*". God decided, by grace to bless Adam, to empower him, to give him the resources even without the assurance of obedience and acceptance of the challenge He gave him.

It's like a father saying to his little child: I paid for it all, go into the biggest toy store and enjoy. Get anything you want! The kid could get a U$1.00 HotWheel, a small toy car, or a stroller car, the kind of plastic electric cart that the boy can drive. It all depends on that boy's decision. It's a matter of believing in the father's promise.

The order of things in Genesis shows that the blessing is upon Adam regardless of any obedience, but the complete fulfillment of the blessings would only be enjoyed in obedience of dominion, multiplication and leadership. God is gracious, loving and doesn't charge us for it. He gave by grace. The promises are free, but all the blessing to a certain point, become useless if we don't apply them in God's order. The promises are free, but they will be weak and aimless without application. The application is simple: act in leadership. Ask for an opportunity in your LifeGroup this week. Multiply disciples wherever you go. Stand. Lead. Multiply...

Jairus versus the woman with the discharge of blood

Let's take a look to the story of Jairus and the woman who had a discharge of blood, narrated in Mark chapter 5 verses 21 to 43. If you remember, we have a man whom the Bible calls Jairus, a ruler of the synagogue. He was a famous, important person. On the way to heal Jairus' daughter, an unnamed woman, without any reference other than her disease, came along. Jesus, here, decided to heal her first. I imagine that Jairus felt offended and even more anxious. It states that, "*Jesus, perceiving in Himself that power had gone out from Him, immediately turned about in the crowd and said, 'Who touched My garments?' And His disciples said to Him, 'You see the crowd pressing around You, and yet You say, '"Who touched me?"' And he looked around to see who had done it.*"   Mark 5:30-32 (ESV).

Think how distressed Jairus became. Maybe he thought, "Why did He stop? Why is He healing this unimportant woman? Who cares about this woman? Come on Jesus, remember my need!". Jesus cared for that woman. Jesus saw her intensity. Jesus notice her touch, and it was different. Jairus and dozens of people were constantly touching Jesus' garments, but that woman received, while many missed their chance to enjoy that incarnated grace named Jesus! How is that possible? That is what many brother and sisters are experiencing today. They miss the chance to properly use grace.

For twelve years that woman had suffered from a discharge of blood and had suffered much under many physicians, and had spent all that she had, and after all this, her illness only grew worse. This was an unclean woman. She could not touch anything or anyone because that thing or person would become unclean as well. Suddenly Jesus says, "Who touched me?" When it was revealed that it was this unclean woman I think that was the test for Jairus, the ruler of the synagogue. Jairus knew the law (Lev. 15:19–23). Would he trust the law of Moses or the grace of Jesus? As a faithful jew, Jairus should not receive the "unclean" Jesus in his house, but Jairus was brought to the same level of intensity as that unnamed woman. Praise God Jairus understood grace.

Once the woman received grace she understood the use of such blessing. Mark 5:33

(ESV) *"But the woman, knowing what had happened to her, came in fear and trembling and fell down before Him and told Him the whole truth."* She used grace and confessed herself as powerless and incompetent to resolve her own issue. She didn't use her healing to boast and start a reckless life. I know there are brothers and sisters who see grace as opportunity for sin, but true grace brings us to repentance and transformation. Real grace leads to the fear of the Lord. Jesus never spoke to the woman with any teaching about repentance, because the real experience with grace always brings transformation. Jesus only said: *"Daughter, your faith has made you well; go in peace, and be healed of your disease."*Mark 5:34.

Now look at Jairus. It seems that he needed to be delivered from the reputation and his fame among the multitude. Jesus had decided to bless him anyway, but on this journey between asking for his daughter's healing and the miraculous manifestation, Jairus learned the futility of reputation. It's just like that. Real grace always change us.

To close this chapter please take a look at the moment when Jesus arrived at Jairus' house. Mark 5:39-40 (ESV) *"And when He had entered, He said to them, 'Why are you making a commotion and weeping? The child is not dead but sleeping.' And they laughed at Him. But He put them all outside and took the child's father and mother and those who were with Him and went in where the child was."* How is it possible that Jairus had people inside of his house that could laugh and joke in such a tragic moment like that one? When I lost my youngest son I learned a precious lesson about the people we should put outside that are inside our house. Not everyone that is crying with you really cares about your suffering.

Jairus was a ruler of the synagogue, a recognized figure. He had many people around him. However the kind of people encircling him, didn't really care about his pain. When Jairus received Jesus in his life, in his house, he allowed Jesus "to put everybody outside". This is what grace should do in your life, change even the kind of people you are used to walking with. Overcomers enjoy grace, allowing it to change everything in their lives.

Jesus healed the girl, and after the blessing, Jesus said, *"give her something to eat."* Mark 5:43. The responsibility comes after the blessing and not before. It was like that with Adam, and also with Jairus. Enjoy grace while using it towards others.

Please pray: *Lord Jesus, we are so grateful for Your love and for Your grace. I ask that You give me a true understanding and clear revelation of this grace. Help me to see others through Your eyes! Make me a channel of Your grace. Help me to receive this blessing and be changed by it. Let it stir me into action and responsibility to follow Your calling.*
Today I pray especially for those people that You bring into our lives and into our church. I pray these souls will be changed and transformed by Your grace. In Jesus name. Amen.

21
OVERCOMERS WILL BE RAPTURED

When I was a new believer one of the most terrifying ideas was the rapture. I knew verses like 1 Thessalonians 4:17, "*Then we who are alive, who are left, will be caught up together with them in the clouds to meet the Lord in the air, and so we will always be with the Lord*". Passages like these should have produced hope and excitement in my heart, but the real feeling was of worry and distress. Mainly passages like "*Then two men will be in the field; one will be taken and one left. Two women will be grinding at the mill; one will be taken and one left. Therefore, stay awake, for you do not know on what day your Lord is coming*". (Matthew 24:40-42).

Will I be awake? Am I going to be prepared? I don't want to be like the ones in Matthew 7:21 who worked in vain. Jesus said "*Not everyone who says to me, 'Lord, Lord,' will enter the kingdom of heaven.*" Think for few minutes about that. We are talking about people who called Jesus their Lord. They did things, religious things. However, those things were probably not the will of God. Jesus completed the idea with *"the one who does the will of My Father who is in heaven"* will enter the kingdom. We have already explained that this kingdom is the reward of the overcomers. This is not salvation, this is being a participant of the rapture.

Here we get the main point: do the will of God. This should be the central target for our existence. What is the will of God? There are maybe hundreds of answers to this question, but I dare to summarize them all by saying what Jesus said in Matthew 28:19 *"Go therefore and make disciples of all nations, baptizing them in the name of the Father and of the Son and of the Holy Spirit"*. All the gifts, all talents and resources should be spent in ways to increase the disciple making process. All other activities should be secondary, if we focus on making disciples.

Some brothers and sisters fear losing their salvation, but the truth is that once you truly give your heart to Jesus absolutely nothing can separate you from the love of God. Romans 8: 35-39 reminds us " *... nothing in all creation, will be able to separate us from the love of God in Christ Jesus our Lord"*. Note that you must be in Christ Jesus to have this assurance. Are you? If yes, great, don't worry about your salvation anymore. It is finished, but what about 1 Corinthians 9:27 that says " *But I discipline my body and keep it under control, lest after preaching to others I myself should be disqualified.* " Notice that Paul was really worried about being disqualified by running aimlessly. If you are running, that means you are saved, but now there is a final line for the overcomers.   We should fix our eyes on Jesus and make disciples to conquer the victory crown. This is not about salvation but about the rapture and the kingdom.

When Paul wrote 1 Corinthians, he was in the beginning of his ministry. The great apostle had a fear at this stage of his life and most of us identify with his concern, but this apprehension did not seem to produce the right fruit in my heart. Instead of feeling a willingness and boldness, most of us feel threatened and afraid. 1 John 4:18 says " *There is no fear in love, but perfect love casts out fear. For fear has to do with punishment, and whoever fears has not been perfected in love.*" A great number of brothers and sisters see the rapture more as a "punishment" than an actual moment of deliverance, but the rapture is salvation from a terrible time that the world will face, not a punishment.

The Apostle John, in his first letter, let us know that love is the key to seeing the rapture as a time of redemption instead of a penalty. Yet I still had problems with fear about this mysterious moment of which no one even knows when it will take place. The feeling of being unprepared, or caught off guard was terrible. I believe that you do not want to fear this moment anymore, right? The way of deliverance is to love this moment. We should pray about this. We should pine over that incredible moment. While you learn how to pray for the rapture keep running, keep fighting, continue making disciples.

In my personal life I have many reasons to desire the rapture more intensely. At the time of writing of this chapter, 132 days have passed since my precious 2 years old son went to heaven. I desire so much to see him again. I miss his sweet face and smile. It seems that after my grieving, heaven became an easier finish line to keep my eyes on. Regardless of all the missing and pain, what I really want is to meet Jesus. I know that in this encounter all pain and grief will be gone. I know that in the end, life will overcome death. I know that an eternal joy is waiting for me.

The rapture has an aspect of judgment related to it, but it is not the main purpose. The rapture is for the joy of all the overcomers. It is the reward for the good and faithful servant (Matthew 25:23). This will be the greatest of all signs the world will ever see, and you and I are invited to be part of this great moment.

Today, the Lord wants to take all fear away and establish hope and great expectation for this event of which no one knows the time that it will happen. The mystery is part of the grand surprise, not of fear. I really don't like surprises. Usually it is because of the lack of control. The sensation that I have lost authority is sometimes horrible, but that's exactly the point of the rapture's mystery. No man, no minister nor preacher can dominate anyone. Only Jesus has the final authority over His church. It will be an amazing surprise for me. I'll love and enjoy it. Are you ready for this surprise moment?

Pray now: *My God, here is my heart again. Today, I decide to set my mind on the things above, the things of heaven, not on earthly things (Colossians 3:2). I believe in miracles, that's why I pray for the restoration of this person's life (mention the person's name). But the greatest restoration of all is still to come. My eyes are fixed on the finish line, on heaven. Lord, help me respond to all of the challenges that are in front of me today. I want to respond as an overcomer. I want to be ready for the rapture, whether the time is favorable or not (2 Timothy 4:2), so give me a chance today, to share Your gospel. Let me have an opportunity to stand for You today. In Jesus' name. Amen.*

ABOUT THE AUTHOR

Raphael was born on August 25, 1982, Raphael Fernandes is a son of a business family. He was ordained to ministry in 2009 but since 2004, he has been full time dedicated to church planting. As a teenager and youth leader, he led around 400 people to a disciple life-style in a local church in Brazil. He was sent in 2011 to the USA to be the lead pastor of a project in Pensacola, FL and in 2012 became the senior pastor of the brand new church, The Vine Fort Myers. With training in missiology (1999 studied at Youth with a Mission) and a heart to teach and make disciples (graduated in Pastoral Ministry at The Vine Biblical Institute – 2009). Pastor Raph is passionate for Southwest Florida and its local culture. He got married to Juliana in 2004 and together have three sons (Andre, Pedro and Joab-who is in heaven). He studied Civil Engineering and has a Physics Bachelor from University Catholic of Goias which made possible 7 years being a high school teacher.

Printed in Great Britain
by Amazon

25439462R00078